HOW TO STOP BEING TOXIC AND BUILD HEALTHY RELATIONSHIPS

BECOME SELF-AWARE, STOP HURTING OTHERS, QUIT MANIPULATIVE AND NARCISSISTIC BEHAVIORS TO BOOST CONFIDENCE AND RESTORE INNER PEACE

TAYLOR BLAKE

NORTH STAR PRESS

CONTENTS

Introduction   v

1. The Anatomy of Toxic Behavior   1
2. Unraveling the Web of Manipulation   24
3. The Path to Self-Insight   48
4. Repairing and Building Healthy Relationships   70
5. Addressing Common Challenges on the Path to Transformation   97
6. Building a Future Free from Toxicity   118
7. Beyond the Mirror: Extending Your Impact   133

Conclusion   145
Also by Taylor Blake   147
References   149

INTRODUCTION

Several years ago, I found myself sitting across from a close friend who, with concern and frustration, listed ways my actions and words had been causing pain to those around me. That moment was a pivotal point in self-discovery. For so long, I had navigated through life unaware of the toxic patterns deeply hidden within the dynamics of my interactions. What made this revelation even more surprising was my profession—I am a life coach, deeply committed to fostering self-awareness and positive change in others. Yet here I was, confronted with the reality that despite my expertise and self-awareness, I had exhibited behaviors others felt were toxic at times. This contradiction between my personal actions and my professional ideals shook me to my core. The journey from that painful acknowledgment to where I stand today was not easy or quick, but it was transformative. This book is born from that journey. It's a testament to the belief that change, though challenging, is profoundly possible. Through sharing this experience, I hope to illuminate the shadows where unconscious patterns hide, even in those who dedicate our lives to guiding others toward their light.

Years after that pivotal conversation, and having successfully applied these strategies to my own life, I have started implementing them with my clients who struggled with the aftermaths of their toxic behavior. Witnessing their

Introduction

transformative effects not just on my clients but also on the lives of their loved ones, I was inspired to write this book. I designed it specifically to aid individuals who, like me, have identified harmful patterns in their actions and are dedicated to evolving. While numerous resources are devoted to spotting toxicity in others, this book is geared towards those courageous enough to introspect, understanding that the initial step towards transformation is self-awareness, which is crucial for breaking free from detrimental cycles. Drawing on years of coaching experience, I am committed to offering practical, evidence-based strategies that can be seamlessly integrated into your daily life.

"Toxic behavior" is a term that encompasses a wide range of actions and attitudes that can harm or manipulate others. Grounded in psychological research and expert insights, we will explore what constitutes toxic behavior and how it manifests in relationships and interactions.

The objectives of this book are clear: to foster self-awareness, to cease manipulative behaviors, to halt the cycle of hurting others, and to cultivate healthy, fulfilling relationships. This journey is not just about ceasing negative behaviors; it's about building a foundation for lasting inner peace and confidence.

Structured into five pivotal sections — Self Awareness and Understanding Toxicity in Yourself, Deconstructing Toxic Behaviors, Building Emotional Resilience, Effective Communication Strategies, and Restoring and Building Healthy Relationships — this book offers a comprehensive roadmap for transformation. Each chapter includes actionable steps, real-world scenarios, and exercises for deep engagement and practical application.

Embarking on this path will require introspection and may challenge long-held beliefs and patterns. Depending on your stage in the transformative journey upon beginning this book, you may experience discomfort while navigating certain sections. However, I urge you not to be discouraged. I assure you that the outcomes of growth and healing awaiting at the end of this journey are profoundly rewarding.

I invite you to turn the page and start the first chapter with an open heart and a willing spirit. The road ahead is not easy, but it is complete with the potential for profound personal growth and the opportunity to forge healthier, more meaningful connections.

Introduction

Let this book be your ally, offering hope, guidance, and reassurance that change is not only possible but within reach. Together, let us step forward into a future defined by healthier relationships, inner peace, and newfound confidence.

1

THE ANATOMY OF TOXIC BEHAVIOR

In the quiet moments of reflection, it's not uncommon to confront aspects of ourselves that we're less than proud of. In these moments, often sparked by feedback from those we value, we're presented with a choice: to defend our actions or take a step back and assess our role in our own lives and the lives of others. This chapter is about making the latter choice, about facing the uncomfortable truth that some of our behaviors may be toxic. It's about recognizing these patterns within ourselves and the commitment to initiate change.

The term "toxicity" has pervaded discussions on interpersonal dynamics and is frequently used to describe behaviors that are harmful or destructive. However, recognizing toxic traits within ourselves requires moving beyond this broad terminology to understand the nuances of our actions and their impacts.

1.1 Understanding Toxicity in Yourself

Self-awareness is the foundation: The first step in addressing any issue is acknowledging its existence. For many, this realization comes after repeated patterns of conflict or feedback from those close to them. Consider a scenario where, after a disagreement at work, instead of reflecting on the feedback given, the immediate response is defensive. This reaction might shield from immediate discomfort but also block the path to growth. Here, honest self-reflection is pivotal. It involves asking hard questions and being ready to hear the answers. It's about objectively looking at one's behavior, even when what we see is hard to face.

The spectrum of toxic behavior: Toxic behaviors don't all look the same; they exist on a spectrum. On one end, there might be subtle habits like frequently interrupting others or not considering different viewpoints. On the more severe end, these behaviors can escalate to manipulation or verbal abuse. Recognizing where one's actions lie on this spectrum is critical. Without this understanding, efforts to change may fall short or miss the mark entirely.

Internal triggers: Behind every action, there's a motive, a driving force. These triggers can be varied, from a deep-seated fear of rejection that leads to controlling behavior to insecurities about one's capabilities that manifest as undue criticism of others. Recognizing these triggers isn't about excusing toxic actions but understanding them from the point of empathy towards oneself. This understanding is the first step towards addressing the root cause rather than just the symptoms.

The impact on self: The repercussions of toxic behavior extend beyond those on the receiving end; they also take a toll on the individual exhibiting these behaviors. This impact might not be immediate or apparent, veiled under the guise of short-term 'wins' like getting one's way. However, the long-term effects can include isolation, strained relationships, and a deteriorating sense of self-worth. It's essential to understand that in harming others, whether through words or actions, one also harms oneself, eroding the very foundations of healthy self-esteem and well-being.

In the process of self-examination and growth, it's crucial to approach oneself with the same compassion and understanding extended to others. This approach doesn't diminish the importance of accountability but recognizes the human capacity for change. The steps towards identifying and addressing toxic traits are not easy or quick, but they are possible. With each small step, the path to healthier behaviors and relationships becomes clearer, guided by the commitment to be better for those around us and ourselves.

1.2 Recognizing Passive and Active Forms of Toxicity

To effectively navigate the complexities of toxic behavior, it is crucial to distinguish between its passive and active manifestations. This distinction aids in self-reflection and sets the stage for targeted personal growth.

Defining Passive Toxicity

Passive toxicity might not grab headlines, but its subtlety does not diminish its impact. It's the withdrawal in response to conflict instead of seeking resolution or the silent treatment as a form of punishment. It's manipulation not through direct actions but through inaction or the withholding of affection, communication, or support. This form of toxicity is insidious, often because it doesn't leave visible marks. Yet, it erodes trust and intimacy, leaving confusion and hurt in its wake.

Defining Active Toxicity

Conversely, active toxicity is unmistakable. It's the raised voice during an argument, the cutting remark meant to belittle, or the blatant disregard for another's boundaries. It includes behaviors like gaslighting, where one party manipulates another into questioning their reality, or verbal abuse, where words are used as weapons. Active toxicity demands attention because its effects are immediate and palpable, casting long shadows over relationships and self-esteem.

The Danger of Normalization

A profound risk lies in the normalization of these behaviors. Consider a scenario where sarcastic remarks at a partner's expense are a common occurrence. Initially, they might elicit laughter or be dismissed. Over time, however, they become a staple of interaction, a norm. In this normalization, the urgency for change diminishes. The behavior becomes woven into the fabric of daily life, its toxic impacts overlooked or rationalized away. This normalization hinders personal growth and solidifies patterns that can be challenging to break.

Identifying Your Toxic Patterns

The path to identification begins with a mirror, not for vanity, but for reflection. It requires an honest assessment of one's behaviors, asking probing questions about the nature of your interactions with others. Are there moments when silence is wielded like a sword, cutting off communication to assert control? Or perhaps instances where words are deployed to diminish rather than uplift?

This process of identification is not about self-flagellation but understanding. It involves recognizing the contexts in which these behaviors emerge. Is withdrawal a response to feeling overwhelmed or threatened? Does aggression surface in moments of insecurity or fear of loss? By pinpointing these patterns and their triggers, you lay the groundwork for meaningful change.

The recognition of passive and active forms of toxicity within oneself can be unsettling. It confronts us with the parts of ourselves we might prefer to ignore or justify. Yet, it is in this confrontation that growth begins. By understanding the nuances of our behaviors and their impacts, we equip ourselves with the knowledge needed to foster healthier ways of relating to ourselves and those around us.

1.3 The Psychological Roots of Manipulative Behavior

Manipulative behavior, while often dismissed as merely cunning or deceitful, is deeply rooted in the psyche. It's not as straightforward as choosing to deceive for personal gain; more often, it's a complex defense mechanism, a learned response to underlying emotional turmoil. To unravel the threads of manipulative behavior, we must delve into the psychological underpinnings that drive individuals to resort to manipulation.

The Need for Control

At the heart of manipulative behavior lies a profound need for control. This urge is not about power in the traditional sense but about creating a predictable, manageable environment. Controlling others or the situation provides a semblance of safety for someone who feels powerless or uncertain. It's a coping strategy, albeit harmful, for dealing with the unpredictability of life. The irony is that in the pursuit of control, one often pushes away those they seek to keep close, creating a self-fulfilling prophecy of loss and isolation.

Fear of Vulnerability

Closely tied to the need for control is the fear of vulnerability. Showing one's true self, with all its flaws and insecurities, is terrifying for someone who equates vulnerability with weakness. Manipulation becomes a protective shield, a way to engage with others while keeping the vulnerable self hidden. It's a tragic paradox that by avoiding vulnerability, one also misses out on the depth of connection and intimacy that comes from genuine, open interactions. The mask of manipulation may protect from immediate pain but at the cost of true connection.

Influence of Past Trauma

To understand manipulative behavior, one must also consider the shadow of past trauma. Early experiences of betrayal, abandonment, or manipulation by caregivers can leave deep scars, teaching the lesson that the world is not to be trusted and that love and attention are commodities to be earned or taken. These experiences shape one's approach to relationships, often leading to a reliance on manipulation to preemptively protect oneself from perceived threats. It's a learned survival tactic, deeply ingrained and challenging to unlearn.

Breaking the Cycle

Acknowledging the psychological roots of manipulative behavior is a crucial step toward change. It requires confronting the pain, fear, and insecurity beneath the surface and understanding that these emotions are at the core of the need to manipulate. This process is neither quick nor easy. It demands patience, courage, and, often, the guidance of a skilled therapist.

However, the act of acknowledgment itself is powerful. It shifts the narrative from blame and shame to understanding and empathy, not just for others but for oneself. It paves the way for healing, allowing for the development of healthier coping mechanisms. Instead of control and manipulation, one learns to seek connection and authenticity, to build relationships on trust rather than fear.

The journey toward breaking the cycle of manipulation is about relearning how to relate to oneself and others. It involves cultivating self-awareness, practicing vulnerability in safe spaces, and gradually replacing manipulative behaviors with more direct, honest forms of communication. It's about learning to find safety not in control but in the unpredictable beauty of genuine human connections.

This change doesn't happen overnight. It's a gradual process filled with setbacks and successes. Yet, with each step forward, the cycle of manipulation loosens, making way for a future built on the solid ground of trust, respect, and authentic connection.

1.4 The Impact of Toxicity on Personal Relationships

Toxic behaviors, whether they manifest as subtle manipulations or overt aggressions, invariably cast long shadows over personal relationships. These shadows, if left unchecked, can grow, obscuring the warmth and light that connections with others can bring into our lives. Understanding the nuanced ways in which toxicity impacts these relationships is not just about recognizing the harm done; it's about acknowledging the steps necessary for healing and growth.

Erosion of Trust

At the core of any strong relationship lies trust. It's the glue that binds individuals together, allowing for vulnerability, growth, and mutual support. However, toxic behaviors act like water seeping through the foundation of a house, slowly but surely eroding this trust. When one party consistently engages in actions that prioritize self-interest over mutual respect, the other starts to question the reliability and safety of the relationship. Whether it's through dishonesty, manipulation, or disrespect, the outcome is the same: a chasm forms where trust once flourished. Rebuilding this trust requires more than just patching over the surface; it necessitates a deep, foundational repair of the behaviors that caused the damage.

Creating a Cycle of Negativity

Toxic behaviors have a peculiarly insidious nature; once introduced into a relationship, they tend to perpetuate a cycle of negativity. This cycle often begins subtly, with small grievances and resentments that go unaddressed. Over time, these accumulate, leading to a climate where negative interactions become the norm rather than the exception. Each party may find themselves reacting not to the immediate situation but to the buildup of past hurts and disappointments. This reactionary stance makes it increasingly difficult to break free from the cycle, as each negative interaction reinforces the pattern, further deteriorating the dynamics of the relationship.

Barriers to Genuine Connection

Human connections thrive on authenticity and openness. These are the elements that allow relationships to deepen, moving beyond superficial interactions to something more meaningful. Toxicity, however, sets up formidable barriers to this depth of connection. When one's actions are guided by manipulation or self-preservation rather than honesty and empathy, it becomes almost impossible to connect on a genuine level. The protective walls built to safeguard against vulnerability also serve to keep others at a distance. Inside these walls, one might feel safe, but it's a solitary kind of safety, devoid of the richness that true connection brings.

The Role of Accountability

Amidst the challenges that toxic behaviors pose to personal relationships, accountability emerges as a beacon of hope. Taking accountability means more than just acknowledging one's toxic actions; it's about understanding the impact of these behaviors on others and committing to change. This process often requires confronting uncomfortable truths about oneself and the ways in which one's actions have harmed others. It's a step that demands courage, for it involves not just facing the past but actively working to ensure a different future.

Accountability acts as a bridge, offering a path back to trust and connection. It signals to those hurt by toxic behaviors that their pain is recognized and valued and that the relationship is worth the effort of repair. This acknowledgment, when coupled with consistent actions that demonstrate change, can slowly start to mend the fractures caused by toxicity. It's a process that doesn't happen overnight, and there may be setbacks along the way. However, each step taken toward accountability is a step away from the cycle of negativity toward a relationship grounded in mutual respect and understanding.

In the realm of personal relationships, the impact of toxicity cannot be overstated. It erodes trust, perpetuates negativity, and creates barriers to genuine connection. Yet, within this landscape of challenges, there exists the potential for transformation. By recognizing the harm caused, taking accountability, and committing to change, it's possible to move beyond toxic patterns. This path isn't easy, nor is it linear, but it is paved with the potential for deeper, more meaningful connections with others.

1.5 How Toxicity Erodes Self-Esteem and Confidence

The effects of toxic behavior extend beyond the immediate harm to others, casting a long shadow on the perpetrator's self-perception and self-worth. This often-overlooked aspect of toxicity reveals a vicious cycle where negative actions towards others diminish one's self-esteem, leading to further toxic behaviors in a misguided attempt to regain control or assert dominance. This section explores the intricate relationship between toxic actions, self-esteem, and confidence, offering insights into breaking this cycle.

The Mirror Effect

When we exhibit toxic behavior towards others—whether through manipulation, aggression, or disrespect—it's akin to throwing mud. While our intention might be to target the other person, we end up soiling our hands in the process. This "mirror effect" reflects our actions back onto us, shaping how we see ourselves. Engaging in harmful behaviors towards others can lead us to internalize negative self-views, seeing ourselves as unworthy of love and respect. This internalization is detrimental to our self-esteem as we begin to define our worth by our worst actions rather than our capacity for kindness, empathy, and growth.

Self-Sabotage

A direct consequence of diminished self-esteem is the tendency to engage in self-sabotage. This can manifest in various aspects of life, from personal relationships to professional opportunities. For instance, someone who feels unworthy might push away loving partners or undermine their success at work, reinforcing their negative self-view. This cycle of self-sabotage is a defense mechanism, protecting the individual from the vulnerability of hope and the fear of failure. However, it also traps them in a state of stagnation, where personal and professional growth is sacrificed at the altar of fear and self-doubt.

The Isolation Spiral

Toxic behavior often leads to a pattern of isolation, both self-imposed and from external sources. As relationships strain or sever due to harmful actions, the individual may find themselves increasingly alone. This isolation reinforces negative self-views, as the lack of positive interactions and feedback loops deprives the individual of external sources of self-esteem and confidence. The spiral deepens as the isolation feeds into a narrative of unworthiness, further eroding self-confidence and making the prospect of reaching out or forming new connections daunting. This isolation not only impacts social well-being but also affects professional networks and opportunities, closing doors that might otherwise lead to growth and improvement.

Pathways to Rebuilding

Breaking free from the cycle of toxicity, self-doubt, and isolation requires intentional actions and a commitment to self-improvement. Here, we explore strategies for rebuilding self-esteem and confidence:

- **Self-Compassion:** Begin with developing self-compassion. Recognize that everyone makes mistakes and that growth is possible. Treat yourself with the same kindness and understanding you would offer a friend in a similar situation.
- **Positive Affirmations:** Implement positive affirmations into your daily routine. Regularly remind yourself of your strengths, accomplishments, and the positive qualities you bring to your relationships and work. This practice can gradually reshape your self-view, highlighting your worth beyond your past behaviors.
- **Seek Feedback:** Engage in conversations with trusted friends or colleagues who can provide honest, constructive feedback. This external perspective can offer insights into your strengths and areas for growth, challenging the internal narrative that may focus exclusively on your faults.
- **Professional Support:** Consider seeking support from a therapist or counselor. Professional guidance can help you navigate the complexities of self-esteem and toxic behavior, offering strategies for healing and self-improvement.
- **New Experiences:** Pursue new experiences and hobbies that challenge you and provide opportunities for success and fulfillment. These activities can bolster your confidence, proving to yourself that you are capable of growth and achievement.
- **Reflective Practices:** Engage in reflective practices such as journaling or meditation. These activities provide space for introspection, helping you to understand your actions, their impacts, and your feelings about yourself in a deeper, more nuanced way.
- **Social Re-engagement:** Gradually re-engage with social activities and networks. Start small, with one-on-one interactions or small groups, and focus on building positive, supportive connections. These relationships can serve as mirrors reflecting your growth and worth, countering the negative self-views cultivated in isolation.

- **Accountability:** Hold yourself accountable for your actions, but do so from a place of growth rather than punishment. Recognize when you fall into old patterns and take proactive steps to correct your course, using these moments as opportunities for learning rather than self-criticism.

Rebuilding self-esteem and confidence after recognizing and addressing toxic behaviors is a journey marked by small, consistent steps forward. It involves shifting the focus from what you have done wrong to what you can do right, from who you have been to who you are becoming. This process is not linear, and setbacks are part of the landscape of change. However, with each positive action, each moment of self-compassion, and each step towards healthier relationships and behaviors, you rebuild the foundation of your self-esteem and confidence, paving the way for a future defined by growth, self-respect, and positive connections.

1.6 The Cycle of Toxic Behavior: Recognition, Reaction, and Repetition

Realizing one's behavior might be toxic is a crucial step, but it marks only the start of a more complex process. The real work begins with the decision to act on this awareness, to shift from acknowledgment to transformation. This section navigates through the subsequent stages: understanding reactions to your acknowledgment, breaking free from the cycle of repetition, and the pivotal role of support systems in facilitating change.

Recognition is Just the Beginning

Identifying toxic traits within oneself is a significant milestone. Yet, the path from recognition to rectification is fraught with challenges. It's akin to diagnosing a disease — understanding the condition is vital, but it's the treatment that leads to recovery. Transitioning from acknowledgment to action requires a steadfast commitment to change and the humility to accept that mistakes have been made. It's a process that demands patience, both with oneself and the process, recognizing that old habits are hard to break and that slip-ups are part of the journey toward healthier behaviors.

Understanding Reactions

When you begin to address your toxic behavior, it's natural to face a spectrum of reactions from those around you. Some may express skepticism, conditioned by past experiences, while others might offer cautious optimism. Managing these reactions involves a delicate balance of empathy and assertiveness. It's crucial to listen actively to their concerns, validating their feelings without allowing their doubts to derail your progress. At the same time, it's beneficial to communicate your intentions clearly — sharing your plans for change and soliciting their support. This open dialogue can help rebuild trust and foster a supportive environment conducive to your growth.

Breaking the Repetition

To dismantle the cycle of toxic behavior, developing new, healthier coping mechanisms is essential. This task can be daunting, as it often means stepping out of comfort zones and confronting uncomfortable emotions head-on. Consider, for instance, someone who has used sarcasm to mask insecurities. For them, a healthier coping mechanism might involve expressing their feelings directly, even if they feel vulnerable. Strategies to facilitate this shift include:

- **Mindfulness practices**: Engaging in mindfulness can help one become more aware of their triggers and responses, offering the clarity needed to choose healthier reactions.
- **Skill-building**: Investing time in learning communication and emotional regulation skills can equip one with the tools needed to handle situations that previously elicited toxic responses.
- **Reflection and journaling**: Regular reflection can help identify patterns in behavior and track progress, while journaling offers a safe space to process emotions and thoughts constructively.

The Importance of Support

The role of a solid support system in breaking the cycle of toxic behavior cannot be overstated. Support can come in many forms — from friends and family who offer a listening ear and encouragement to professionals like therapists or counselors who provide guidance and strategies for change. This network serves as a safety net, offering both accountability and affirmation. For example, a friend might gently point out when old patterns resurface, offering a timely reminder of the commitment to change. Meanwhile, a therapist can help navigate the deeper-seated issues driving toxic behavior, offering personalized strategies for overcoming them.

Engaging with support groups, either in-person or online, can also be incredibly beneficial. These communities offer a sense of belonging and understanding, providing a platform to share experiences, challenges, and successes with individuals who are on similar paths. This collective wisdom not only enriches one's journey but also reinforces the idea that change, though difficult, is achievable.

The process from recognizing toxic behavior to implementing and sustaining change is not linear. It involves navigating a complex web of emotions, reactions, and setbacks. However, with a commitment to change, understanding the reactions it may provoke, strategies to avoid repetition, and a solid support system, breaking free from the cycle of toxic behavior is within reach. This path demands perseverance, empathy, and an unwavering belief in the possibility of transformation.

1.7 Differentiating Between Being Toxic and Having a Bad Day

In human emotions and behaviors, distinguishing between what constitutes toxicity and what simply reflects a bad day is crucial. This differentiation not only aids in self-awareness but also in fostering self-compassion and understanding towards oneself and others. It's about grasping that the fabric of our interactions is woven with threads of myriad colors, not just black and white.

Normalizing Human Imperfection

Human beings are inherently flawed, a truth that, while universally acknowledged, often gets lost in the discourse around toxic behavior. Everyone, at some point, snaps at a colleague, utters words in anger, or withdraws into silence. These moments, though regrettable, are part of being human. They stem from stress, fatigue, or the countless pressures life throws our way. Recognizing this imperfection is about understanding that a bad day doesn't define our character. It's a moment in time, not a lifetime. This acknowledgment serves as a foundation for self-compassion, allowing us to treat ourselves with the same kindness we would offer a friend in a similar situation.

The Pattern Makes It Toxic

The true hallmark of toxicity lies not in singular actions but in patterns of behavior. It's the difference between a single overcast day and a perpetual storm. Toxic behavior is characterized by repeated, consistent actions that harm others, whether through manipulation, aggression, or neglect. These are not isolated incidents but a series of choices that form a discernible pattern over time. Identifying these patterns requires honest reflection and, often, feedback from others. It's about looking beyond the surface to see the recurring themes in one's actions and their impacts on those around us. This process, while challenging, is essential in moving from recognition to change.

Self-Forgiveness

Self-forgiveness plays a pivotal role in differentiating between being toxic and having a bad day. It's about acknowledging the mistake, understanding its impact, and committing to doing better, all while extending kindness to oneself. Self-forgiveness doesn't mean excusing harmful behavior or diminishing its effects on others. Rather, it's about breaking the cycle of guilt and self-recrimination that often follows a bad day. By forgiving yourself, you open the door to growth and healing, allowing yourself to move forward with a clearer understanding of your actions and a renewed commitment to positive change. It's a delicate balance between accountability and compassion, a balance that fosters resilience and self-awareness.

Maintaining Perspective

Keeping a balanced perspective on one's behavior is crucial in navigating the complex terrain of human interactions. This involves recognizing the difference between a moment of weakness and a deeper issue that needs addressing. It's about seeing the forest for the trees, understanding that while everyone has moments they're not proud of, these don't necessarily indicate a toxic pattern. Maintaining this perspective requires regular self-reflection and, when needed, seeking feedback from trusted individuals who can offer an outside view. This balanced approach allows individuals to address their mistakes without losing sight of their overall growth and progress.

Understanding the nuances of human behavior is key in navigating the journey from recognizing toxic behavior to fostering healthy relationships and self-improvement. It involves taking responsibility for one's actions that cause harm to others while also acknowledging and forgiving oneself for the unavoidable mistakes made simply by virtue of being human. This nuanced approach encourages a balanced perspective, fostering a deeper understanding of oneself and paving the way for genuine transformation.

1.8 The Role of Childhood and Past Trauma in Shaping Toxic Behaviors

Childhood, the foundation upon which our adult selves are built, holds the keys to many of the behaviors we exhibit later in life. The experiences and traumas we endure as children don't just fade away; they embed themselves into our psyche, influencing how we navigate the world as adults. Recognizing the roots of toxic behaviors in these early experiences is crucial for anyone seeking to understand and rectify their actions.

Unpacking Childhood Influences

The environments we grow up in, the relationships we observe, and our interactions with caregivers and significant adults all play pivotal roles in shaping our behavioral blueprint. For instance, a child who witnesses constant conflict or criticism in their household may internalize these patterns, believing them to be normal ways of communication. This normalization can inadvertently set the stage for toxic behaviors in adulthood, as these learned patterns are replicated in future relationships.

Similarly, childhood traumas such as neglect, abuse, or abandonment leave deep imprints. These experiences can instill a deep-seated fear of vulnerability or a perpetual insecurity. In an attempt to protect oneself from further hurt, one might adopt toxic behaviors as defense mechanisms, pushing others away with hostility or manipulation to avoid the pain of potential rejection or betrayal.

The Replication of Learned Behaviors

The replication of behaviors learned in childhood is often a subconscious process. It's not a deliberate choice to hurt others but a learned survival tactic. Take, for instance, the individual who resorts to manipulation to meet their needs. This strategy might have been learned from observing caregivers who used manipulation as a tool to control their environment. Without conscious intervention, these learned behaviors continue to manifest in adult relationships, perpetuating a cycle of toxicity that can be difficult to break.

Recognizing the source of these behaviors is the first step toward change. It involves reflecting on one's upbringing and the behaviors modeled by those around them. This reflection can be challenging, as it often brings painful memories to the surface. However, it also offers valuable insights into the origins of one's toxic behaviors, providing a roadmap for change.

Healing the Child Within

Breaking free from the cycle of replicating learned toxic behaviors requires healing the wounds of the past. This process, often referred to as healing the inner child, involves acknowledging and addressing the pain and trauma experienced in childhood. Here are some strategies that can facilitate this healing:

- **Therapy:** Engaging with a therapist can provide a safe space to explore childhood traumas and their impact on current behaviors. Therapies such as cognitive behavioral therapy (CBT) or eye movement desensitization and reprocessing (EMDR) are particularly effective in addressing trauma.
- **Self-compassion:** Practicing self-compassion is crucial during this healing process. It involves treating oneself with kindness and understanding, recognizing that the behaviors learned in childhood were coping mechanisms developed for survival.
- **Reparenting:** Reparenting involves giving oneself the love, care, and guidance that may have been lacking in childhood. This can include setting healthy boundaries, practicing self-care, and nurturing one's emotional and physical well-being.
- **Mindfulness and meditation:** These practices can help cultivate a sense of presence and awareness, allowing one to recognize when they are slipping into old patterns and choose healthier responses.

The Power of Understanding

Understanding the role of childhood experiences and traumas in shaping toxic behaviors empowers individuals to change their narrative. It shifts the perspective from one of blame — either towards oneself or one's caregivers — to one of understanding and growth. With this understanding comes the realization that while the past cannot be changed, the future is still unwritten.

Armed with this knowledge, you can make conscious choices about how you wish to behave, relate to others, and view yourself. It allows for creating a new identity, not defined by past traumas or learned behaviors but by who you choose to become. This shift doesn't negate the challenges or the pain of the past but positions them as stepping stones toward a healthier, more fulfilled self.

In this context, the change process becomes not just about shedding toxic behaviors but about reclaiming one's sense of self. It's about acknowledging where you have come from and deciding where you wish to go. This journey, though highly personal, speaks to a shared experience of resilience, growth, and change that we all have the potential for.

1.9 Self-Assessment: Identifying Your Toxic Traits

Self-awareness is the cornerstone of personal growth, requiring an honest look into one's behaviors and patterns. The process of self-assessment, while challenging, opens the door to understanding and, ultimately, transformation. This section offers guidance on navigating this critical step, from creating a conducive environment for self-examination to interpreting feedback and setting intentions for change.

Creating a Safe Space for Self-Examination

Before diving into self-assessment, it's crucial to establish an environment that fosters openness and honesty without judgment. This space, whether it's physical or mental, should be a safe haven where you can openly explore your vulnerabilities without worrying about being judged or being too hard on yourself. To achieve this:

- Set aside dedicated time free from distractions where reflection can occur uninterrupted.
- Approach this process with kindness towards yourself, recognizing that the goal is growth, not self-punishment.
- Consider starting with a meditation or deep breathing exercise to center yourself and reduce any initial resistance or anxiety.

Creating this safe space is an act of self-care, a necessary foundation for the following introspective work.

Tools for Self-Assessment

Several tools and methods can aid in the self-assessment process, each offering a unique lens through which to view one's behaviors and patterns:

- **Journaling:** This powerful tool allows for exploring thoughts and behaviors over time. Writing without censorship can uncover patterns that may not be immediately apparent, revealing the triggers and circumstances that often precede toxic behaviors.
- **Feedback from Trusted Individuals:** Inviting input from friends, family, or colleagues who have your best interests at heart can provide an external perspective on your behaviors. Choose individuals who are likely to offer honest, constructive insights.
- **Self-Assessment Quizzes and Tools:** Numerous online resources and quizzes are designed to help identify toxic traits. While not a substitute for deeper psychological assessment, they can serve as a starting point for self-reflection.

Select the tools that resonate with you, understanding that the most effective method is often a combination of several approaches.

Interpreting Feedback

Receiving feedback on one's behavior can be challenging, especially when it highlights areas for improvement. To effectively interpret and utilize feedback:

- Listen actively, seeking to understand the perspective being offered rather than preparing a defense or rebuttal.
- Reflect on the feedback received, considering how it aligns with your self-assessment and your observed patterns.
- Recognize the value of external insights in painting a fuller picture of your behaviors and their impacts on others.
- Approach feedback with gratitude, understanding that it's offered to support your growth, even if it's difficult to hear.

When approached with openness and a willingness to learn, feedback becomes a powerful ally in the journey towards self-improvement.

Setting Intentions for Change

Identifying toxic traits is only the first step; what follows is the commitment to addressing and transforming these behaviors. Setting clear intentions for change involves:

- Defining specific behaviors you wish to transform and understanding why they're harmful to yourself and others.
- Establishing realistic, achievable goals for change, breaking down larger objectives into smaller, manageable actions.
- Committing to the process of change, recognizing that setbacks are part of growth and not indicators of failure.
- Regularly revisiting and adjusting your intentions as you progress, ensuring they remain aligned with your overarching goals for personal development.

Setting intentions involves moving from recognition to action, from awareness to transformation. It's a commitment not just to cease harmful behaviors but to foster healthier ways of interacting with the world.

In embarking on the path of self-assessment, you engage in an act of courage. It's a process that demands honesty, vulnerability, and a willingness to confront uncomfortable truths. Yet, it's also an opportunity to understand yourself more deeply, grow beyond past limitations, and build a foundation for healthier, more fulfilling relationships and interactions. By creating a safe space for reflection, utilizing diverse tools for self-assessment, interpreting feedback with openness, and setting clear intentions for change, you lay the groundwork for a journey of continuous self-discovery and improvement. This process, while personal and unique to each individual, shares a common goal: the transformation of toxic patterns into behaviors that uplift both oneself and those around us.

1.10 From Acknowledgment to Action: The First Steps to Change

Recognizing toxic traits within ourselves marks a pivotal moment; it's an act of bravery that prepares us for transformation. Yet, this recognition alone does not catalyze change. True progress demands that acknowledgment be paired with concrete action. The transition from understanding one's toxic behaviors to actively modifying them calls for a series of deliberate and thoughtful steps.

Acknowledgment is Not Enough

The initial step of admitting to yourself that certain behaviors are harmful and toxic is critical. However, this acknowledgment serves as the starting line, not the finish. The real work begins when one decides to apply this awareness in a practical sense, committing to altering these behaviors. Consider this: if realization were sufficient, the transformation would be instantaneous and universal. Yet, the path from insight to changed behavior is complex, requiring more than just an internal acknowledgment. It demands a plan of action, a series of steps, and strategies designed to facilitate this shift from toxic patterns to healthier interactions.

Small Steps Lead to Big Changes

The prospect of changing ingrained behaviors can seem overwhelming, akin to standing at the base of a mountain and looking up. The key to making this journey manageable is to break it down into smaller, attainable steps. When consistently applied, these small changes accumulate over time, leading to significant transformation. This approach aligns with the principle of kaizen, a Japanese concept focusing on continuous, incremental improvement. By adopting this mindset, one can make progress without becoming overwhelmed by the magnitude of the task at hand. For instance, if you identify a tendency to interrupt others as a toxic trait, a small step might be to practice active listening in your daily conversation. This manageable change, over time, can significantly alter how you engage in discussions, fostering respect and understanding in place of disruption and dominance.

The Role of Commitment

Committing to the process of change is fundamental. This commitment is the anchor, keeping one grounded when the process becomes challenging or setbacks occur. It's essential to recognize that change, especially when it involves altering deep-seated behaviors, is seldom linear. There will be moments of backsliding, times when old patterns resurface despite your best efforts. In these moments, commitment is what propels you forward, reminding you of the reasons behind your decision to change. This commitment sustains motivation, encouraging persistence even when progress seems slow or imperceptible.

Commitment also implies a readiness to embrace discomfort. Change is uncomfortable by its nature; it challenges existing paradigms and forces you out of your comfort zone. Embracing this discomfort as a necessary part of growth can make the process more manageable. It helps to reframe discomfort not as a sign of failure but as evidence of progress, a marker that you are pushing boundaries and moving towards your goal.

Seeking Accountability and Support

No one exists in isolation, and this truth holds, especially when it comes to personal growth and change. Seeking accountability and support from others can significantly enhance one's ability to stick to their commitment to change. Accountability partners or support groups offer a structure of encouragement and feedback, providing motivation and perspective. These relationships create a space where one can share their successes and challenges, receiving guidance and support in return.

An accountability partner, for example, can serve as a mirror, reflecting one's actions and progress, offering praise for achievements, and gently pointing out when old patterns resurface. This external perspective is invaluable, as it can be challenging to maintain objectivity about one's behavior. Similarly, support groups, whether in-person or online, offer a community of individuals on similar paths. These groups provide a sense of belonging and understanding, reducing the isolation that can come with attempting to change entrenched behaviors.

Furthermore, seeking support from professionals, such as therapists or counselors, can provide tailored strategies to address the root causes of toxic behaviors. These experts can offer insights and techniques that might not be accessible through personal reflection or peer support alone. They can guide one through the complexities of change, helping to navigate the emotional and psychological hurdles that often accompany the process.

In taking the first steps from acknowledgment to action, one embarks on a path marked by self-reflection, commitment, and incremental change. This path, though challenging, is enriched by the support and accountability offered by others, making the journey towards transformation not just possible but sustainable. Through deliberate action, persistent effort, and the embrace of a support network, the shift from toxic behaviors to healthier patterns of interaction can be achieved, paving the way for more fulfilling and respectful relationships with oneself and others.

1.11 The Importance of Professional Help in Addressing Toxicity

Navigating the complexities of personal change can often feel like deciphering an intricate map without a compass. In such moments, professional help serves as a guiding light, illuminating paths that may have remained hidden and offering tools to traverse the terrain of self-improvement with greater ease and understanding.

When to Seek Professional Help

Recognizing the point at which to seek professional assistance is a pivotal step in managing toxicity. Signs that indicate this need may include:

- A persistent sense of unhappiness or dissatisfaction in relationships despite efforts to change.
- Repeatedly falling into the same harmful patterns of behavior without understanding why.
- Feeling overwhelmed by emotions or reactions that seem disproportionate to the situation at hand.
- Experiencing significant distress or disruption in daily life, work, or relationships due to one's behavior.

These indicators suggest that the roots of toxic behavior may be deeper and more complex than initially perceived, necessitating the expertise of a mental health professional to untangle.

The Benefits of Therapy

Engaging in therapy provides a multitude of benefits for those looking to address and transform toxic behaviors. At its core, therapy offers a safe, confidential space where thoughts and feelings can be expressed without fear of judgment or reprisal. This environment fosters deep self-reflection and learning, enabling individuals to:

- Gain insights into the origins of their toxic behaviors, understanding how past experiences and traumas may influence current actions.
- Develop new coping strategies that are healthier and more constructive, replacing old patterns that harm oneself and others.
- Enhance emotional intelligence, including the ability to manage and express emotions in ways that foster rather than damage relationships.
- Build resilience against future stressors, equipping individuals with the tools to handle challenges without reverting to toxic behaviors.

The therapeutic relationship itself is a powerful agent of change. Working with a therapist can model healthy, respectful interactions, providing a real-time framework for how to relate to others in a non-toxic manner.

Overcoming Stigma

Despite the clear benefits, the decision to seek therapy is often hindered by societal stigma. This stigma, rooted in misconceptions and outdated beliefs about mental health, can evoke feelings of shame or weakness. However, challenging this stigma is crucial. Seeking therapy is an act of strength and self-respect. It signifies a commitment to personal growth and the well-being of oneself and those around them.

To combat stigma, consider:

- Educating oneself and others about the true nature of therapy and its role in fostering mental and emotional health.
- Sharing personal stories of therapy, if comfortable, to normalize the experience and demonstrate its benefits.
- Reminding oneself that seeking help is a proactive step toward improvement, not an admission of defeat.

Finding the Right Therapist

The effectiveness of therapy is significantly influenced by the relationship between the therapist and the client. Finding a therapist who is a good fit is therefore essential. Consider the following when searching for a therapist:

- **Specialization:** Look for therapists who specialize in areas relevant to your needs, such as relationship issues, emotional regulation, or trauma.
- **Therapeutic Approach:** Familiarize yourself with different therapeutic approaches (e.g., cognitive-behavioral therapy, psychodynamic therapy) and consider which might best align with your personality and goals.
- **Comfort and Compatibility:** The therapeutic relationship should feel comfortable and safe. Initial consultations can be a good way to gauge compatibility.
- **Logistics:** Consider practical aspects such as location, availability, and cost. Many therapists now offer online sessions, providing flexibility and accessibility.

Maximizing the benefits of therapy involves:

- Being open and honest in sessions. The more you're willing to share, the more your therapist can help.
- Actively participating in the process. Therapy is a collaborative effort that requires engagement both in and out of sessions.
- Implementing strategies and insights gained from therapy into daily life. Real change occurs through the consistent application of new skills and perspectives.

Engaging with a mental health professional is a valuable step for anyone committed to overcoming toxic behaviors. This support not only aids in understanding and addressing the underlying causes of these behaviors but also develops the skills necessary for lasting change. Whether navigating the initial steps of recognizing toxicity or seeking to deepen personal growth, professional help can significantly enhance the journey toward healthier, more fulfilling interactions with oneself and others.

2

UNRAVELING THE WEB OF MANIPULATION

Imagine walking through a dense forest where every step forward is met with a tangled web of vines, making progress difficult. This is what navigating through manipulative behaviors can feel like—every action and word meticulously designed to entangle and control. Understanding the anatomy of manipulation is like finding a machete to clear these obstructions, allowing for healthier and more direct paths of communication.

Manipulation, often cloaked in the guise of concern or affection, can be challenging to recognize—both in others and ourselves. This section sheds light on the signs of manipulative behavior, differentiates it from assertiveness or persuasion, and offers insights into its impact on relationships. Moreover, it encourages a mirror to be held up to one's actions, fostering a culture of honesty and self-awareness.

2.1 The Anatomy of Manipulation: Recognizing the Signs

Defining Manipulative Behaviors

At its core, manipulation is about control. It's using emotional levers to influence others' actions or decisions, not for mutual benefit, but for one's gain. Unlike assertiveness, which respects boundaries and seeks open, honest communication, manipulation operates in the shadows. It's persuasion at the expense of another's autonomy.

- **Guilt-tripping** involves making someone feel overly responsible for your emotional well-being, steering them to act in your favor out of obligation rather than choice.
- **Gaslighting** is the act of making someone question their reality, memory, or perceptions, thus gaining power over them.
- **Emotional blackmail** is the threat of withdrawing emotional support or love to compel someone to comply with your demands.

Understanding these tactics is the first step in recognizing manipulation, both in interactions with others and in reflecting on personal behavior patterns.

Common Tactics of Manipulation

Manipulative behaviors can manifest in various ways, each designed to tip the scales of emotional power in favor of the manipulator. Recognizing these tactics in action can illuminate moments where communication veers from healthy to harmful.

- **Silent treatment:** Withholding communication to exert control or punish.
- **Feigning innocence:** Pretending ignorance or confusion to avoid accountability.
- **Playing the victim:** Overemphasizing personal suffering to gain sympathy and leverage over others.

These behaviors, when left unchecked, weave a complex web that can ensnare relationships in cycles of misunderstanding and mistrust.

The Impact on Relationships

The toll of manipulative behaviors on relationships is profound. At its heart, manipulation erodes the foundation of trust that relationships need to thrive. When hidden agendas drive actions, it leaves little room for genuine connection or mutual respect. The result is often a relationship built on shifting sands, where instability and insecurity become constant companions.

For instance, consider the impact of gaslighting on a partner's self-esteem and trust. Over time, being made to question their reality can lead to a profound sense of isolation and self-doubt, fundamentally altering the dynamics of the relationship.

Self-Reflection on Manipulative Tendencies

Turning the lens inward to examine personal behaviors for signs of manipulation requires courage and honesty. It's about asking hard questions:

- Have there been times when words or actions were designed to control or influence others' choices covertly?
- In moments of conflict, were tactics like silent treatment or guilt-tripping used to gain the upper hand?

Reflecting on these questions can be uncomfortable, but it's a necessary step toward cultivating healthier ways of relating to others. It involves acknowledging past actions without self-condemnation, understanding their impact, and committing to change.

For self-reflection:

- **Journaling**: Writing about instances where manipulative tactics were used can offer insights into triggers and motives. Reflect on what drove those actions and how they affected relationships.
- **Feedback**: Seeking honest feedback from trusted friends or family about how your behavior impacts them can provide an outside perspective, helping to identify patterns that may not be evident from the inside.
- **Professional Guidance**: Sometimes, the roots of manipulative behavior run deep, intertwined with past trauma or deeply ingrained coping mechanisms. In such cases, working with a therapist can offer the tools and support needed to unravel these complex behaviors and work towards healthier relational patterns.

Recognizing and addressing manipulative behavior is no small feat. It demands introspection, a willingness to confront uncomfortable truths, and a commitment to fostering relationships grounded in respect and honesty. By identifying the signs of manipulation and understanding its impact on connections with others, the path toward more authentic and fulfilling interactions becomes clearer. It's about cutting through the dense undergrowth of control and coercion, allowing for relationships where openness and mutual respect can flourish.

2.2 Guilt-tripping: Dynamics and Psychological Impacts

Guilt-tripping operates under the surface of many interactions, a subtle yet powerful tool for manipulation. It taps into the deep-seated human desire to maintain harmony and avoid conflict, leveraging guilt to influence others' actions and decisions. This exploration peels back the layers of guilt-tripping, illuminating its workings and effects.

Understanding Guilt-tripping

At its heart, guilt-tripping is about leveraging someone's capacity for empathy and their ethical or moral standards to sway their behavior. It's a form of emotional manipulation that exploits the sense of obligation or responsibility one person feels towards another. The manipulator may insinuate or directly claim that not acquiescing to their wishes would make the other person selfish, uncaring, or neglectful. The underlying psychological mechanism involves triggering a sense of guilt to override the other's boundaries or desires, leading to compliance.

Identifying Guilt-tripping in Interactions

Spotting guilt-tripping requires attentiveness to the subtleties of communication. Signals include:

- Statements pointing out how much the manipulator has done for you, implying that refusal would be ingratitude.
- Remarks that aim to make you feel selfish for prioritizing your needs or desires.
- Emotional withdrawal or sulking as a punishment for not complying, suggesting you're to blame for any resulting sadness or disappointment.

These indicators, often wrapped in the guise of care or connection, reveal the manipulative intent to make one feel indebted and thus more pliable to influence.

The Psychological Impact of Guilt-tripping

The psychological impact of guilt tripping is significant and multifaceted. Those subjected to it may experience:

- A noticeable erosion in self-esteem, as they are made to feel inadequate or at fault for their feelings or actions.
- Heightened levels of anxiety and stress, resulting from the constant pressure to appease the manipulator's demands and avoid inducing guilt.
- A pervasive sense of self-doubt, as the guilt-tripping undermines their decision-making confidence, trapping them in a cycle of seeking the manipulator's approval.

These consequences highlight the importance of recognizing and addressing guilt-tripping, as it can lead to enduring emotional and psychological harm.

Strategies for Overcoming the Tendency to Guilt Trip Others

For those recognizing a pattern of guilt-tripping in their behavior, change is both necessary and achievable. Strategies include:

- **Mindfulness and Self-Reflection:** Cultivate an awareness of the emotions driving the urge to manipulate. Reflect on the need these actions are attempting to fulfill and consider healthier, more direct ways of communicating these needs.
- **Develop Empathy:** Focus on understanding and empathizing with others' feelings and perspectives. This can help shift the approach from manipulation to mutual respect.
- **Practice Direct Communication:** Instead of implying or insinuating, practice expressing needs and desires openly and respectfully. This fosters honest dialogue and reduces the reliance on guilt to influence others.
- **Seek Feedback:** Engage close friends or family members in your efforts to change, asking them to point out when your behavior leans towards manipulation. This external perspective can be invaluable in recognizing and modifying your actions.
- **Professional Support:** If guilt-tripping is deeply ingrained or linked to broader emotional issues, seeking help from a therapist

can provide the tools and guidance needed to alter these patterns.

Moving away from guilt-tripping towards healthier interaction patterns not only improves relationships but also enhances one's sense of integrity and self-respect. It shifts the dynamic from control and obligation to one of genuine connection and mutual respect.

2.3 Gaslighting: A Deep Dive into Its Mechanisms and Impacts

In the realm of toxic behaviors, gaslighting stands out for its insidious nature and profound impact on individuals. It is a form of manipulation that seeks to sow seeds of doubt in a person's perceptions, memories, or beliefs, effectively disorienting and controlling them. This tactic, when employed, can erode the very foundation of one's sense of reality, making it a particularly destructive form of psychological manipulation.

Understanding Gaslighting

At its core, gaslighting is about power and control. By casting doubt on the validity of someone's experiences or feelings, the gaslighter gains a superior position, steering the narrative to their advantage. This manipulative tactic can be subtle, such as questioning the memory of an event, or overt, like outright denial of an occurrence that definitely took place. The aim is to make the victim question their sanity, which, in turn, makes them more dependent on the gaslighter for their version of reality.

Identifying Gaslighting in Interactions

Realizing you might be gaslighting others involves carefully examining how you interact with them. Signs that you could be engaging in gaslighting include:

- Often finding yourself doubting or second-guessing others' recollection of events.
- Noticing that people seem confused or disoriented during or after conversations with you.
- Regularly dismissing or downplaying others' emotions as overreactions or untrue.
- Observing that people around you feel isolated or believe their experiences are not validated or taken seriously by you.

For those who may unknowingly gaslight others, reflections on interactions can reveal tendencies to dismiss others' feelings or to assert control by undermining their reality.

The Psychological Impact of Gaslighting

The repercussions of gaslighting on mental health are profound and far-reaching. Victims may experience:

- A significant decrease in self-confidence and self-trust, as constant questioning leads them to doubt their judgment and perceptions.
- Increased anxiety and depression stemming from the confusion and isolation gaslighting produces.
- A sense of helplessness and dependency on the gaslighter for validation and reality checks.

These effects underscore the need for recognition and intervention, as gaslighting can lead to long-term emotional and psychological distress.

Strategies for Counteracting Gaslighting

For those who recognize they have engaged in gaslighting, whether intentionally or not, several strategies can foster change:

- **Acknowledge and Accept Responsibility:** The first step is to own up to the behavior without excuses. This acknowledgment is crucial for change.
- **Understand the Root Causes:** Reflect on what drives the need to gaslight. Is it fear of vulnerability, a desire for control, or something else? Understanding these motivations is key to addressing the behavior.
- **Seek Professional Help:** Therapy can be instrumental in unraveling the complexities behind gaslighting behavior, offering tools and strategies for healthier interaction patterns.
- **Practice Open and Honest Communication:** Commit to expressing needs and feelings transparently, without resorting to manipulation. This includes active listening and validating others' experiences and perceptions.
- **Build Empathy:** Actively work on understanding and empathizing with others' feelings and perspectives. This can help shift the focus from control to connection.

In understanding and addressing gaslighting, the focus shifts from undermining reality to fostering an environment where open, honest communication and mutual respect are paramount. This shift not only counteracts the damaging effects of gaslighting but also lays the foundation for healthier, more authentic relationships.

2.4 Emotional Blackmail: Exploring the Shadows of Emotional Coercion

In interpersonal relationships, emotional blackmail is a covert dance of power where one person uses emotional triggers to coerce another into compliance. This manipulation tactic disrupts the equilibrium of relationships and erodes the core of individual autonomy and respect.

Clarifying Emotional Blackmail

At its essence, emotional blackmail manipulates the emotional strings of guilt, fear, and obligation to control another's actions. It transforms love, care, and concern into weapons of compliance, where the victim feels trapped between their values and the manipulator's demands. For example, a partner might suggest their love is conditional on specific behaviors or decisions, subtly implying or overtly stating that deviation from these expectations will result in emotional withdrawal or punishment.

Spotting Patterns of Emotional Blackmail

Recognizing emotional blackmail within oneself is essential for self-improvement and healthier relationships. This process involves introspection and acknowledging when your actions manipulate others' emotions to meet your needs. Signs to watch for include:

- Utilizing guilt, fear, or obligation as tools to influence others' decisions or behaviors. Did your partner ever mention feeling like they must "walk on eggshells" to avoid upsetting you?
- Resorting to threats, ultimatums, withholding affection, or playing the victim to elicit sympathy and control the situation.
- Noticing a pattern where your compliance with your demands leads to short-term peace but long-term resentment and disempowerment from your partner.

Admitting these behaviors can be challenging but is crucial for personal growth and building connections based on mutual respect rather than manipulation. It requires a willingness to understand the deep-seated reasons behind these actions and to seek healthier communication and conflict-resolution methods. By recognizing and addressing these tendencies, you open the door to more genuine and respectful interactions.

Countermeasures for Those Using Emotional Blackmail

For individuals who recognize a tendency to engage in emotional blackmail, transforming this pattern begins with self-awareness and a commitment to change. Strategies include:

- **Reflecting on Needs and Desires:** Identify what you are trying to achieve through emotional blackmail. Understanding these underlying needs allows for the pursuit of more direct and healthy communication strategies.
- **Practicing Assertive Communication:** Learn to express needs, desires, and feelings openly and directly, without resorting to manipulation. Assertive communication fosters clarity and understanding, paving the way for genuine connection.
- **Developing Empathy:** Cultivating an understanding of how your actions affect others can shift your approach from manipulation to cooperation, recognizing the value of respecting others' autonomy and decision-making.

Embarking on this path of change not only enhances personal integrity but also enriches relationships with deeper trust and respect.

Safeguarding Against Emotional Blackmail

Protecting oneself from the grips of emotional blackmail involves developing resilience and self-assurance, enabling you to stand firm in your values and decisions. Strategies for fortification include:

- **Recognizing Your Rights:** Affirm your right to your feelings, opinions, and decisions, irrespective of external pressure. This foundational belief acts as a shield against manipulation, grounding you in your autonomy.
- **Setting Clear Boundaries:** Define and communicate your limits

clearly and consistently. Boundaries are essential for healthy interactions, signaling respect for personal space and autonomy.
- **Seeking Support:** Surround yourself with a supportive network that validates your experiences and offers perspective. This circle can provide strength and validation, reminding you of your worth and right to respectful treatment.
- **Building Self-Esteem:** Cultivate a strong sense of self-worth independent of others' approval or actions. A robust self-esteem serves as armor against attempts to manipulate your emotions or decisions.

By embedding these practices into your daily life, you create a resilient foundation that not only deflects attempts at emotional blackmail but also fosters a climate of mutual respect and understanding in your relationships.

In navigating the complex terrain of emotional blackmail, the journey from recognition to resolution is paved with self-reflection, commitment to change, and the cultivation of healthy relational skills. Whether you find yourself on either side of this dynamic, understanding its mechanisms and impacts is the first step towards fostering relationships characterized by authenticity, respect, and mutual support.

2.5 Control vs. Influence: Redefining Interpersonal Dynamics

In the intricate dance of human relationships, the line between guiding and governing can blur, leading to a tangle of interactions driven by control rather than influence. This distinction, subtle yet profound, shapes the fabric of our connections, coloring them with shades of respect and autonomy or shadowing them in hues of dominance and submission. Here, we unravel this distinction, exploring the undercurrents that drive the desire to control and charting a course toward positive influence.

Differentiating Control from Influence

To navigate through life's relationships, understanding the divergence between control and influence is crucial. Control seeks to direct the actions and decisions of others, often disregarding their wishes or autonomy. Influence, on the other hand, is about inspiring or guiding others through one's actions or example, respecting their freedom to choose. While control tightens the reins, influence opens the gates, fostering an environment where ideas can flourish and decisions are made collaboratively. This distinction is not merely semantic; it defines the very essence of our interactions.

- **Control** manifests in directives, demands, and decisions made with little regard for the other's input.
- **Influence** operates through persuasion, inspiration, and encouragement, valuing the other's perspective and choice.

Acknowledging this difference is the first step in shifting from a dynamic of dominance to one of mutual respect and cooperation.

The Desire for Control

Peeling back the layers, the impulse to control often stems from a labyrinth of personal insecurities, fears, and past experiences. These driving forces, deeply rooted, can push individuals towards seeking dominion over others as a means of compensating for internal turmoil or perceived threats.

- **Insecurity** might manifest as a need to control to assert one's value or importance.
- **Fear** of uncertainty or loss can drive individuals to grip tightly to the reins, attempting to manage every outcome.
- **Past experiences**, particularly those involving loss of control or trauma, can condition a response that equates control with safety.

Understanding these motivations is pivotal, not for justification, but for addressing the underlying issues that fuel the need for control.

Shifting Towards Positive Influence

Transitioning from controlling behaviors to becoming a positive influence is a metamorphosis that requires introspection, effort, and a genuine desire for change. This shift involves:

- **Self-awareness:** Cultivating an understanding of your behaviors and their impacts. Recognizing moments of control and reflecting on their roots can illuminate pathways to change.
- **Empathy:** Fostering an ability to understand and share the feelings

of others. Empathy bridges gaps, allowing for a deep connection that influence, rather than control, can nurture.
- **Open Communication:** Practicing transparency in expressing your thoughts and feelings encourages a reciprocal openness, laying the groundwork for influence built on trust rather than fear.
- **Modeling Behavior:** Leading by example is a potent form of influence. Demonstrating the qualities you admire, like resilience, kindness, or integrity, can inspire those around you more effectively than any directive.

By embodying the principles you advocate, you become a powerful source of influence, guiding through example rather than decree.

Building Relationships on Respect and Trust

The cornerstone of any enduring relationship is a foundation constructed on mutual respect and trust. This bedrock, once established, supports interactions that are enriching, authentic, and free from the shadows of control.

- **Mutual Respect:** Acknowledging and valuing the autonomy and opinions of others fosters a climate of respect. It's in this space that relationships can thrive, unencumbered by the weight of control.
- **Trust:** Cultivating trust involves consistency in words and actions, reliability, and a commitment to transparency. Trust diminishes the need for control as confidence in the other's decisions and capabilities grows.

These pillars, respect and trust, are not erected overnight. They are built through daily actions and choices that prioritize understanding and collaboration over dominance and unilateral decisions. It's in this environment that true influence can blossom, where guidance is offered with open hands rather than imposed with clenched fists.

The journey from control to influence is paved with challenges, requiring a dismantling of long-held beliefs and behaviors. Yet, it is a path worth traversing, for at its end lies the potential for relationships that are not only healthier but infinitely more rewarding. In these connections, driven by positive influence, we find the true essence of interpersonal dynamics, where each interaction is a thread woven into a tapestry of mutual respect and shared growth.

2.6 The Role of Insecurity in Driving Manipulative Behavior

Insecurity, often hidden beneath layers of outward confidence or masked by a veneer of control, can significantly influence one's interactions, leading to the adoption of manipulative behaviors. These behaviors, while seemingly serving as a protective mechanism, ultimately stem from an inner dialogue marked by doubt and self-criticism. Recognizing and addressing these insecurities helps us grow personally and builds stronger, more authentic relationships.

Linking Insecurity to Manipulation

Insecurities act as the silent drivers behind the wheel of manipulation, steering actions and words in directions that safeguard perceived vulnerabilities. When individuals feel threatened, inadequate, or fearful of rejection, manipulation can emerge as a strategy to assert control or create a facade of emotional security. This behavior, however, is a double-edged sword. While it may offer temporary relief or a semblance of control, it erodes trust and intimacy, the very elements necessary for secure and fulfilling relationships.

Recognizing Insecurity Within

The journey to recognizing one's insecurities begins with mindful observation of one's reactions and behaviors. Signs that insecurities may be influencing behavior include:

- A tendency to overreact to criticism or perceived slights.
- Frequent comparison of oneself to others leads to feelings of inadequacy.
- A pattern of sabotaging relationships or opportunities out of fear of failure or rejection.

Identifying these signs requires an honest and compassionate self-assessment. It's about observing without judgment and acknowledging vulnerabilities as part of the human experience.

Addressing and Overcoming Insecurities

Transforming the role insecurities play in one's life involves a multifaceted approach, focusing on internal growth and the development of healthier coping mechanisms.

- **Self-reflection:** Dedicate time to introspection, exploring the origins of your insecurities. Understanding their roots can demystify their power over your actions.
- **Therapy:** Engaging with a therapist can provide a structured approach to addressing insecurities. Therapy offers a safe space to explore vulnerabilities, with guidance to develop strategies for overcoming them.
- **Building self-esteem:** Cultivate a practice of self-compassion and affirmation. Celebrate your strengths and accomplishments, however small they may seem. Building self-esteem is about rewriting the narrative of self-worth, focusing on inherent value rather than external validation.
- **Expanding comfort zones:** Challenge yourself by stepping into situations that stretch your comfort zones. Each successful experience serves as a building block for confidence, reducing the impulse to resort to manipulation as a defense mechanism.

These strategies, while simple in concept, require persistence and patience. It's a gradual process of rewiring long-held beliefs and behaviors, with progress measured in small victories and insights.

Transitioning to Secure and Healthy Interactions

Moving from insecurity-driven manipulation to secure, healthy ways of interacting is a transformation that benefits not only oneself but also those with whom one interacts. The transition involves:

- **Practicing authenticity:** Strive for honesty in your expressions and actions. Authenticity fosters genuine connections, reducing the need for manipulative behaviors.
- **Active listening:** Cultivate the skill of active listening, showing genuine interest in others' thoughts and feelings. This practice can validate both your experiences and those of others, creating a foundation of mutual respect.
- **Vulnerability:** Allow yourself to be vulnerable with trusted individuals. Vulnerability, though risky, can lead to deeper

connections and understanding, mitigating the need for control through manipulation.
- **Effective communication:** Develop clear and effective communication skills. Clearly expressing needs and desires can prevent misunderstandings and foster an environment of openness.

This transition is not about perfection but progress, embracing growth, and learning from setbacks. It's a commitment to evolving one's approach to interactions and choosing paths marked by honesty, respect, and empathy.

In the realm of personal growth, addressing the insecurities that fuel manipulative behaviors is a profound step toward cultivating relationships rooted in trust, respect, and genuine connection. This process, while challenging, illuminates the strength inherent in vulnerability and the power of authentic interactions. As we navigate our insecurities and transform our behaviors, we open doors to more fulfilling and honest connections, marking a departure from the shadows of manipulation towards the light of genuine interaction.

2.7 Shifting from Manipulation to Assertiveness

Assertiveness is a golden middle path in communication, striking a balance between passivity and aggression. It is the art of expressing one's thoughts, feelings, and needs directly and respectfully. Unlike manipulation, which thrives on the exploitation of emotions and vulnerabilities, assertiveness fosters an environment of transparency and equality. The benefits of embracing assertiveness touch both the communicator and the receiver, leading to interactions characterized by honesty and mutual respect.

Assertive communication, in essence, liberates individuals from the exhausting cycle of manipulation. It eliminates the need to read between lines or decipher hidden meanings, laying the groundwork for straightforward and genuine exchanges. This directness not only clarifies intentions but also builds a foundation of trust—a cornerstone of lasting relationships.

Tools for Developing Assertiveness

The road to assertiveness is paved with intention and practice. Several tools and techniques can aid in this transformation:

- **"I" Statements:** Learn to frame your messages from your perspective, focusing on your feelings, thoughts, and needs. For example, instead of saying, "You never listen to me," try, "I feel unheard when my opinions are overlooked."
- **Clear Boundaries:** Understand your limits and communicate them clearly. Boundaries are personal and can vary widely; what's important is that they are expressed openly and respected mutually.
- **Active Listening:** This involves fully engaging with the speaker, showing genuine interest, and confirming understanding before responding. It's a vital component of assertive communication, ensuring that exchanges are not just heard but comprehended.
- **Rejection Management:** Learn to accept 'no' without viewing it as a personal attack. Assertiveness allows for the expression of needs and desires but also respects the other party's right to decline.

Incorporating these tools into daily interactions gradually shifts the dynamic from one of control or submission to one of equality and respect.

Practicing Assertiveness in Daily Life

Real-world application cements understanding and fosters growth. Consider these scenarios for practice:

- **At Work:** If you consistently overstep boundaries with a colleague at work, consider how your actions might affect them. It's helpful to approach them with an "I" statement, explaining your awareness of the impact and openly discussing a boundary you aim to respect moving forward.
- **In Personal Relationships:** When discussing plans or needs, articulate your desires openly, listen to the other's perspective, and seek a compromise that respects both parties.
- **In Conflict Situations:** Instead of resorting to silence or aggression, express your feelings and viewpoint directly, striving for a resolution that acknowledges both sides.

Each of these instances provides an opportunity to strengthen assertive habits, encouraging both personal authenticity and mutual respect.

The Impact of Assertiveness on Self-Image and Relationships

The ripple effects of assertiveness extend far beyond the moment of communication. Adopting an assertive stance reshapes not only how others perceive you but also how you see yourself. It instills a sense of self-respect and empowerment, knowing that you can express your needs and feelings without undermining those of others. This self-assurance fosters a positive self-image, reinforcing the belief in one's worth and the validity of one's feelings and needs.

In relationships, assertiveness lays down the pillars of trust and respect. It eliminates the guesswork and gamesmanship of manipulation, creating a transparent and open environment where each individual feels seen and valued. This foundation enables relationships to flourish, grounded in honesty and mutual understanding.

By transitioning from manipulation to assertiveness, you unlock a realm of communication where authenticity reigns. This shift not only enhances personal well-being but also enriches the tapestry of your relationships, weaving patterns of trust, respect, and mutual support. Assertiveness, therefore, is not just a skill but a gateway to a life characterized by genuine connections and self-respect.

2.8 Handling the Urge to Control: Strategies for Letting Go

Control, a compelling force, often stems from a wellspring of fear and a longing for security. It's a natural instinct to seek stability in the unpredictable currents of life. However, when the desire to control overshadows the ability to trust and empower, it becomes a barrier to genuine connections. The path to releasing this grip involves understanding its origins, embracing mindfulness, empowering those around us, and celebrating autonomy within our relationships.

Understanding the Urge to Control

The impulse to control situations or others doesn't emerge in a vacuum. It's deeply rooted in individual experiences and emotional landscapes. Common catalysts include:

- A history of instability or unpredictability leads to a craving for order and predictability.
- Fear of the unknown or unexpected drives a need to micromanage environments and relationships to prevent perceived threats.

- Feelings of inadequacy or vulnerability, where control becomes a shield against potential harm or hurt.

Acknowledging these underlying causes is a critical step. It shifts the focus from the symptoms of controlling behavior to its emotional and psychological underpinnings, allowing for more targeted and effective interventions.

Mindfulness and Letting Go of Control

Mindfulness, the practice of being present and fully engaged with the current moment without judgment or distraction, offers a powerful antidote to the urge to control. It fosters an awareness of our thoughts and feelings, providing the space to observe the impulse to control without acting on it. Techniques include:

• **Breathing exercises**: Simple yet effective, focusing on your breath can anchor you in the present, reducing anxiety and the need to control.

• **Observation exercises**: Dedicate moments to simply observe your surroundings without seeking to change or influence them. This practice cultivates acceptance and the ability to let go.

Incorporating mindfulness into daily routines can gradually ease the compulsion to control, replacing it with a sense of peace and acceptance.

Empowering Others Instead of Controlling Them

Shifting from control to empowerment involves a fundamental change in how we view and interact with others. It's recognizing their capability to make decisions, solve problems, and manage their lives. Empowerment strategies include:

- **Offering support**: Provide guidance and support when asked, rather than imposing unsolicited advice or direction.
- **Encouraging autonomy**: Celebrate and encourage independent thought and action. Acknowledge others' abilities to navigate their challenges.
- **Fostering a growth mindset**: View mistakes and setbacks as opportunities for learning and growth, both for yourself and others, reinforcing the value of experiences over control.

This shift not only enhances the well-being and confidence of those around us but also enriches our relationships with a sense of mutual respect and trust.

Celebrating Autonomy in Relationships

At the heart of healthy relationships lies the celebration of each individual's autonomy—mutual recognition and respect for one's right to self-determination. This celebration involves:

- **Respecting decisions:** Honor the choices and decisions of others, even when they diverge from your own preferences or expectations.
- **Encouraging exploration:** Support loved ones in exploring their interests, passions, and paths, even if they venture into unknown territories.
- **Valuing differences:** Embrace and value the differences in perspectives, experiences, and approaches within your relationships. These differences enrich rather than diminish the connection.

By celebrating autonomy, we not only foster deeper, more trusting relationships but also cultivate an environment where each person can thrive as their true self.

Through understanding the roots of our need for control, practicing mindfulness, empowering those around us, and celebrating autonomy, we can untangle the complex web of control that constrains our relationships and personal growth. This process is not about losing power but gaining the freedom to engage with life and our loved ones in ways that are open, authentic, and deeply connected.

2.9 Apologizing for Past Manipulations: A Step-by-Step Guide

In the realm of personal growth and relationship repair, the art of apologizing holds a pivotal place. It's a gesture that, when executed with sincerity and understanding, can mend the fabric of strained relationships, paving the way for healing and deeper connection. This section aims to dissect the anatomy of a genuine apology, guiding you through acknowledging harm, expressing remorse, and committing to change. Additionally, it explores the delicate process of seeking forgiveness and using apologies as a springboard for personal development.

The Importance of Apologies in Healing Relationships

Apologies, when offered genuinely, have the power to disarm conflict, soothe hurt feelings, and restore dignity to the injured party. They serve as an acknowledgment of wrongdoing, a validation of the other person's feelings, and a crucial step toward reconciliation. In cases where manipulative behaviors have eroded trust and intimacy, a heartfelt apology becomes not just a courtesy but a necessity. It signals a willingness to take responsibility for one's actions and a commitment to do better, laying the groundwork for rebuilding trust and connection.

Crafting a Genuine Apology

A genuine apology is composed of several key components, each serving a distinct purpose in the healing process:

- **Acknowledgment of Harm:** Start by explicitly acknowledging the specific actions or words that caused harm. Avoid vague statements that fail to address the heart of the issue.
- **Expression of Remorse:** Express sincere regret for the pain caused. This involves not just saying "I'm sorry" but conveying an understanding of the impact your actions had on the other person.
- **Commitment to Change:** Demonstrate a commitment to change by outlining concrete steps you plan to take to avoid repeating the hurtful behavior. This shows that your apology is not just words but a pledge to improve.

Crafting an apology that incorporates these elements requires introspection, empathy, and a genuine desire to mend the damage done.

Receiving Forgiveness and Moving Forward

Seeking forgiveness is a vulnerable act, and it's important to approach it without expectations. The process may unfold over time, and the response may vary according to the depth of hurt and the individual's readiness to forgive. Key considerations include:

- **Respect the Other Person's Response:** Understand that forgiveness cannot be demanded or rushed. It's a personal process that everyone navigates in their own time.

- **Give Space:** Allow the other person the space to process your apology and what it means for them. This might mean stepping back and giving them time to reflect.
- **Be Prepared for a Range of Responses:** Be ready to accept any outcome, from immediate forgiveness to a need for more time or even a decision that the relationship cannot be repaired.

Navigating this phase with grace and understanding underscores the sincerity of your apology and respect for the other person's feelings.

Using Apologies as a Catalyst for Personal Growth

Beyond mending relationships, the act of apologizing serves as a powerful catalyst for self-reflection and growth. It encourages a deep dive into one's behaviors and motivations, promoting a shift from defensive justifications to a posture of learning and openness. By taking responsibility for past manipulations and committing to change, you embark on a path of personal development characterized by increased emotional intelligence, empathy, and healthier communication skills. This evolution not only benefits your relationships but also contributes to a more authentic and fulfilling life.

- **Reflect on the Underlying Causes:** Use the process of apologizing to explore why you resorted to manipulation in the first place. What insecurities or fears were at play? Understanding these can help prevent future missteps.
- **Commit to Continuous Improvement:** View your apology as the beginning, not the end, of your growth journey. Embrace ongoing self-improvement, seek feedback, and adjust your behaviors as needed.
- **Foster Empathy:** Let the experience deepen your empathy for others. By fully grasping the impact of your actions, you become more attuned to the feelings and needs of those around you, paving the way for more compassionate interactions.

In navigating the complexities of apologizing for past manipulations, remember that sincerity, empathy, and a genuine commitment to change are your guiding principles. This journey, though fraught with challenges, holds the promise of renewed connections, personal transformation, and a deeper understanding of what it means to interact with honesty and respect.

2.10 Rebuilding Trust: Long-Term Strategies After Manipulation

The fabric of trust, once torn by manipulative actions, requires time, patience, and genuine effort to mend. The path to restoring this trust is not straightforward; it winds through acknowledgment, understanding, and consistent, visible change. The challenges inherent in this process are significant, yet not insurmountable, with focused strategies and a commitment to authenticity.

The Challenges of Rebuilding Trust

The primary hurdle in rebuilding trust lies in overcoming the shadow of past actions. Manipulative behaviors, by their nature, sow doubt and foster insecurity, leaving scars on relationships that can be sensitive to the touch. The memory of these actions can linger, casting a long shadow over efforts to demonstrate change. This backdrop makes the task of rebuilding trust a delicate endeavor, requiring an understanding that trust must be earned anew, not simply expected to return with time.

Steps to Rebuilding Trust

A strategic, step-by-step approach can guide the process of rebuilding trust, focusing on consistency, transparency, and the cultivation of patience:

- **Open Communication:** Initiate conversations that address past behaviors and their impacts openly. Acknowledge the hurt caused and express a genuine desire to make amends. This communication should be ongoing, not a one-time event.
- **Consistent Actions:** Demonstrate change through consistent actions over time. Small, positive behaviors can slowly accumulate to rebuild a foundation of trust. This might include following through on commitments, being punctual, and showing respect in all interactions.
- **Transparency:** Offer transparency in your actions and intentions. This might mean sharing plans, thoughts, and feelings more openly than before, providing reassurance through visibility.
- **Patience:** Recognize that trust rebuilds at its own pace. Pressuring

others to trust you again can be counterproductive. Show understanding and give them the space and time they need.

Monitoring Your Behavior

Self-monitoring plays a crucial role in this process. Continuously reflect on your behavior and its alignment with your goals of trustworthiness and integrity. This involves:

- **Self-Reflection:** Regularly evaluate your actions and their impacts on others. Are you living up to your commitments to change?
- **Seeking Feedback:** Actively seek feedback from those affected by past behaviors. Listen to their perceptions of your actions and use this feedback to guide further improvement.
- **Adjusting Behaviors:** Be willing to adjust your behaviors based on reflection and feedback. This adaptability shows a commitment to doing what it takes to rebuild trust.

Professional guidance, such as therapy, can be invaluable in navigating the complexities of rebuilding trust. Therapists can offer neutral perspectives, strategies for change, and the support and accountability you will need. This professional input complements personal efforts, offering a structured approach to addressing the underlying issues and facilitating genuine, lasting change. In the painstaking process of rebuilding trust, the combination of strategic efforts, self-awareness, and professional support paves a path forward. Through this dedicated approach, it's possible to restore the bonds of trust, transforming relationships into stronger, more resilient connections.

3

THE PATH TO SELF-INSIGHT

In a world that never pauses, where every tick of the clock ushers in a new demand for our attention, the act of turning inward can sometimes feel like a luxury we can scarcely afford. Yet, it's within these quiet moments of reflection that we find the keys to unlocking our most authentic selves. This chapter is not just about looking in the mirror; it's about understanding the reflection staring back at us.

Self-awareness is the bedrock upon which we build a life of intention and meaning. It's the quiet observer within us, noting our patterns of thought, our reactive habits, and the motivations that propel us forward or hold us back. By cultivating this inner awareness, we chart a course towards not only personal growth but also towards deeper, more meaningful connections with those around us.

3.1 The Mirror of Self-Awareness: Reflecting on Your Actions

The Role of Introspection

Introspection is akin to turning on a flashlight in a dark room. Suddenly, aspects of ourselves that were hidden come into focus, revealing the cobwebs of outdated beliefs or the dust-covered dreams we've neglected. It asks us to be both the inquirer and the respondent, to question why we react a certain way in stressful situations or why certain comments trigger a defensive response.

- **Daily Check-ins:** Allocate a few minutes each day for self-reflection. This could be a quiet moment with your morning coffee or a brief pause before bed. Use this time to ask yourself: "What felt good today? What didn't? Why?"
- **Emotion Tracking:** Keep a simple log of your emotional states throughout the week. Note what events or interactions triggered these emotions and any patterns you observe.

Creating a Feedback Loop

A feedback loop in the context of self-awareness means actively seeking and integrating feedback from our environment and the people within it to refine our understanding of ourselves. It transforms introspection into a dynamic process, bridging the gap between how we see ourselves and how others perceive us.

- **Ask for Feedback:** Choose a trusted friend or family member and ask them for honest feedback on a specific behavior or pattern you're working on. Make it clear you're seeking constructive input, not reassurance.
- **Reflect on Feedback:** Sit with the feedback you receive. It might be uncomfortable, but it's in this discomfort that growth occurs. Ask yourself, "What truth can I find in this? How can I use this to improve?"

The Impact of Denial

Denial acts like a fog, clouding our ability to see ourselves clearly. It whispers that we don't need to change, that our actions are always justified. But in denying our flaws and mistakes, we deny ourselves the opportunity for genuine growth and connection. Recognizing and confronting our denial is a crucial step in the journey towards self-awareness.

- **Identify Denial:** Pay attention to moments when you find yourself justifying or rationalizing your behavior. Ask, "Am I being honest with myself, or am I avoiding an uncomfortable truth?"

- **Seek Perspectives:** Sometimes, seeing ourselves through the eyes of others can pierce through the fog of denial. Engage in conversations that challenge your viewpoints, and be open to seeing yourself from a different angle.

Practical Steps for Enhanced Self-Reflection

Self-reflection transforms abstract concepts into tangible practices. Here are some exercises designed to deepen your self-awareness:

- **Mindfulness Meditation:** Start with 5 minutes a day of mindfulness meditation, focusing on your breath and observing your thoughts without judgment. This practice enhances your ability to notice your internal landscape.
- **Journaling:** Keep a journal for your thoughts, feelings, and observations about yourself. Prompt yourself with questions like, "What challenged me today, and how did I respond? What can I learn from this?"
- **Visualization:** Visualize a recent situation where you reacted in a way you're not proud of. Replay the scene in your mind, but this time, imagine handling it in a way that aligns with your values. This exercise helps in bridging the gap between current behaviors and desired ones.

These practices are not one-off tasks but ongoing commitments to nurturing a deeper relationship with ourselves. Through regular introspection, creating feedback loops, confronting denial, and engaging in practical self-reflection exercises, we embark on a path of continuous self-discovery. This journey doesn't promise to be easy, but it offers the profound reward of living a life that's true to our deepest selves, enriched by relationships grounded in authenticity and mutual understanding.

3.2 Emotional Intelligence: The Key to Understanding Yourself and Others

Emotional intelligence (EI) serves as a guiding light, illuminating the path to not only understanding the depths of our own emotions but also navigating the complex emotional landscapes of those around us. It is this keen sense of emotional awareness and control that can elevate our personal and professional lives to heights previously unimagined.

EI encompasses a broad spectrum of skills, each interwoven to enhance our capacity to recognize, comprehend, and manage our own emotions while adeptly interpreting and responding to the emotions of others. At its core, EI is structured around five pivotal pillars: self-awareness, self-regulation, motivation, empathy, and social skills. Together, these components forge a powerful toolset for enhancing interpersonal relationships, elevating work performance, and amplifying overall life satisfaction.

The journey toward heightened emotional intelligence begins with a solid foundation in self-awareness. This pillar calls for an introspective look into our emotional responses, recognizing patterns and triggers that shape our reactions. It's about asking, "What emotions am I feeling, and why?" This inquiry lays the groundwork for the subsequent pillars, each building upon the last to create a comprehensive framework for emotional mastery.

Self-regulation involves taking the reins of our emotions and steering them in directions that align with our goals and values rather than being at the mercy of fleeting feelings. This skill lets us pause before reacting, choosing responses that contribute to positive outcomes.

Motivation, another critical component, drives us to pursue our goals with zest and perseverance. It's the inner fire that fuels our journey toward achievement and fulfillment, powered by a clear understanding of what truly matters to us.

Empathy, the ability to understand and share the feelings of another, is perhaps the most transformative aspect of EI. It allows us to step into the shoes of others, to see the world through their eyes, and to feel the weight of their emotions. This profound understanding fosters deeper, more meaningful connections, bridging gaps and healing divides.

Finally, social skills enable us to navigate the social world with finesse, building relationships, resolving conflicts, and communicating effectively. These skills ensure that our interactions are not just transactions but opportunities for genuine connection and growth.

The Benefits of High EI

The rewards of cultivating high emotional intelligence are manifold. In personal relationships, it enhances our ability to communicate effectively, resolve conflicts, and deepen connections. At work, it can transform our approach to leadership, teamwork, and problem-solving, setting the stage for success and satisfaction. On a broader scale, high EI contributes to a richer, more fulfilling life experience marked by resilience, understanding, and joy.

Developing Empathy

Empathy doesn't always come naturally but can be nurtured and developed through intentional practice. Strategies for enhancing empathy include:

- **Active Listening**: Truly listen to what others are saying, both verbally and non-verbally. Pay attention to their words, tone, and body language, seeking to understand their perspective fully.
- **Perspective Taking**: Regularly challenge yourself to consider situations from another's point of view. This can be as simple as imagining how a friend feels about a recent life change or as complex as considering the motivations behind a colleague's actions.
- **Engage with Diverse Experiences**: Expose yourself to stories, cultures, and experiences different from your own. Books, films, and conversations can all be windows into other lives, expanding your capacity for empathy.

Enhancing Your EI

Enhancing each component of emotional intelligence requires dedicated effort and practice. Consider these targeted exercises:

- **For Self-Awareness**: Keep an emotion diary, noting your feelings throughout the day and reflecting on their triggers and impacts. This can heighten your awareness of your emotional landscape.
- **For Self-Regulation**: Develop a 'pause practice' by taking a moment to breathe and reflect before responding to emotional triggers. This space can allow for more measured and constructive reactions.
- **For Motivation**: Set personal goals that align with your values and passions. Break these down into actionable steps and celebrate your progress, however small.
- **For Empathy**: Practice the exercises outlined above, focusing on active listening and perspective-taking. Volunteer work can also be

a powerful way to develop empathy by connecting with others' experiences.
- **For Social Skills:** Engage in role-playing exercises that simulate social scenarios, from casual conversations to conflict resolution. Feedback from peers can provide valuable insights into your social interaction style and areas for improvement.

In weaving these practices into the fabric of our daily lives, we not only enhance our emotional intelligence but also unlock the potential for more meaningful and satisfying life experiences. Through this dedicated cultivation of EI, we equip ourselves with the tools not only to navigate the complexities of human emotion but also to thrive within them, fostering a world marked by deeper understanding and connection.

3.3 The Power of Mindfulness in Combatting Toxicity

Mindfulness, often misconceived as a mere trend, holds profound implications for our mental, emotional, and relational well-being. At its essence, mindfulness invites us to experience the present moment without judgment, fully engaging with our current experience. This practice, far from passive, is an active endeavor to anchor ourselves amidst life's storms, offering clarity and calm in places once dominated by impulsivity and reactivity.

In the context of toxic behaviors, which thrive on unexamined reactions and unchecked emotions, mindfulness emerges as a potent antidote. It equips us with the tools to pause and reflect, rather than react, enabling a transformation in how we navigate our inner landscapes and interact with the world around us.

Reducing Reactivity

Toxic behaviors often spring from a place of reactivity, where our actions are more reflex than choice. Mindfulness interrupts this cycle, inserting a pause between stimulus and response. This pause is where choice lies, and with choice comes the power to change. By cultivating mindfulness, we learn to recognize our automatic reactions—be it anger, defensiveness, or withdrawal—and assess whether they serve us and our relationships well. Over time, this practice diminishes our tendency towards these reactive patterns, fostering responses that align more closely with our values and aspirations.

Mindfulness Exercises

Incorporating mindfulness into daily life can be both simple and profound. Here are exercises designed to enhance emotional awareness and regulation:

- **Focused Breathing**: This foundational exercise involves concentrating on your breath and following its journey in and out of your body. When your mind wanders, gently bring it back to your breath. This practice can serve as an anchor, bringing you back to the present moment.
- **Sensory Engagement**: Engage deeply with one of your senses at a time. For example, when eating, focus fully on the taste, texture, and smell of your food. This exercise heightens your awareness and appreciation of the present.
- **Mindful Movement**: Whether walking, stretching, or practicing yoga, move with intention and awareness. Notice the sensations in your body, the rhythm of your breath, and how each movement feels.
- **Body Scan**: Lie down and mentally scan through your body, starting from your toes and moving upwards. Notice areas of tension or discomfort without judgment, simply observing and acknowledging your physical sensations.

These exercises, when practiced regularly, can profoundly impact our emotional landscape, offering a sanctuary of calm and clarity amidst the chaos of daily life.

The Long-term Benefits of a Mindful Practice

The benefits of a sustained mindfulness practice extend far beyond the immediate calm it can provide. Over time, individuals who engage regularly with mindfulness report:

- **Reduced Stress**: By focusing on the present and disengaging from cyclical, stress-inducing thoughts about the past or future, mindfulness significantly lowers stress levels.
- **Improved Relationships**: Mindfulness enhances our ability to listen and engage with others without judgment, fostering deeper

connections and reducing conflict.
- **Increased Self-awareness:** Regular mindfulness practice cultivates an increased awareness of our thoughts, feelings, and reactions, enabling us to understand ourselves better and change unhelpful patterns.
- **Emotional Regulation:** Mindfulness aids in managing difficult emotions, reducing instances of reactivity and impulsivity, hallmarks of toxic behavior.

In essence, mindfulness offers a pathway to a more centered, peaceful, and compassionate existence. It invites us to experience life more fully, to appreciate the richness of the present moment, and to engage with ourselves and others in a way that is mindful, deliberate, and kind.

Through focused breathing, sensory engagement, mindful movement, and body scans, we develop the capacity to step back from the brink of reactivity and to choose how we respond to the world around us. This choice is the heart of mindfulness—a gentle but powerful reminder that, in every moment, we have the opportunity to choose kindness, patience, and understanding, both for ourselves and others.

3.4 Developing Empathy: Understanding the Impact of Your Actions

Empathy, often confused with sympathy, plays a pivotal role in enhancing our ability to connect with others on a deeper level. While sympathy might involve feeling pity or sorrow for someone's situation, empathy goes a step further. It's about stepping into another person's shoes, seeing the world through their eyes, and feeling what they feel. This distinction is crucial, as empathy fosters a genuine understanding and connection, moving beyond mere acknowledgment of someone's distress to a shared emotional experience.

In the tapestry of human relationships, empathy acts as a vital thread, weaving connections that are based on a profound understanding and mutual respect. It's the bridge that narrows the gap between individuals, allowing for a flow of genuine compassion and support. When we operate from a place of empathy, our interactions transform. We begin to approach conversations with a curiosity about the other person's perspective, leading to interactions that are not just exchanges of information but opportunities for true connection.

One of the most effective methods for developing empathy is through active listening. This practice is about fully concentrating on what is being said, rather than passively 'hearing' the message of the speaker. Active listening involves:

- **Giving full attention to the speaker**, avoiding distractions and refraining from formulating your response while the other person is still talking.
- **Acknowledging the speaker's perspective**, even if you disagree. This can involve nodding your head, saying "I understand," or paraphrasing what has been said to show that you are engaged.
- **Responding appropriately**, which means offering feedback that indicates you have genuinely considered the speaker's point of view.

Practicing active listening can significantly enhance your empathetic skills, as it encourages an open and non-judgmental approach to conversations, making the other person feel valued and understood.

However, developing empathy is not without its challenges. Bias and judgment can act as barriers, clouding our ability to truly empathize with someone. These challenges often stem from our own preconceived notions and experiences, which can color our perception of others' situations. To overcome these barriers:

• **Challenge your assumptions** by reminding yourself that your perspective is not the only valid one. Acknowledge that your experiences, values, and beliefs are not universal.

• **Seek out diverse perspectives** to broaden your understanding of people's lives and experiences. This can involve engaging with stories, media, and conversations that expose you to viewpoints different from your own.

• **Practice humility**, recognizing that empathy requires us to admit that we don't always have the answers or fully understand someone else's experience. It's about learning to be comfortable with the discomfort that sometimes comes with stepping into another's emotional world.

Empathy is not a static trait but a skill that can be cultivated and strengthened over time. By actively engaging in practices that enhance our empathetic abilities and confronting the challenges that arise, we pave the way for more meaningful and fulfilling relationships. Through empathy, we not only deepen our connections with others but also enrich our own emotional lives, opening ourselves up to a broader range of human experiences and emotions.

3.5 Emotional Regulation: Strategies to Manage Your Reactions

Emotions ebb and flow like the tide, a natural part of being human. However, when they surge uncontrollably, they can lead to reactions we later regret. The art of emotional regulation involves recognizing our emotional triggers, the very catalysts of these surges, and learning to navigate our responses in a way that aligns with who we aim to be.

Identifying Emotional Triggers

Our journey through emotional landscapes begins with identifying the signposts—our triggers. These are specific situations, words, or actions that evoke a strong emotional response, often rooted in past experiences or deeply held beliefs. Pinpointing these triggers is akin to mapping the terrain of our emotional world, offering us insight into why we react the way we do.

- **Reflect on past reactions:** Think about recent instances when you felt overwhelmed by emotion. What was happening around you? Who was involved? Identifying common themes can help pinpoint your triggers.
- **Listen to your body:** Often, our bodies notice triggers before our minds do. A quickened heartbeat, a knot in the stomach—these physical cues can signal an emotional response is underway.

The Role of Pause

In the space between stimulus and response lies our power to choose. This pause is a crucial tool in emotional regulation, allowing us to step back and assess the situation before reacting. It's in this brief interlude that we can ask ourselves, "Is my impending reaction in line with my values? Is there a more constructive response?"

- **Implement the 5-second rule:** When you feel a strong emotion rising, count to five. This brief interval can provide the distance

needed to choose a more measured response.
- **Use a mantra**: Having a go-to phrase can help center you during emotionally charged moments. It could be as simple as "This too shall pass" or "I choose how I react."

Strategies for Calming the Mind

At times, our emotions can feel like a whirlwind, leaving us seeking shelter in the storm. Various techniques can help calm our minds, offering refuge and clarity.

- **Breathing techniques**: Deep, controlled breathing signals to your body that it's time to relax. Try inhaling for a count of four, holding for seven, and exhaling for eight.
- **Visualization**: Picture a place that evokes peace and calm within you. It could be a quiet beach at sunset or a cozy nook in your home. Immerse yourself in this place, engaging all your senses to deepen the experience.
- **Grounding exercises**: When emotions threaten to carry you away, grounding exercises can bring you back to the present. Focus on tangible sensations - the feel of your feet on the ground, the texture of an object in your hand.
- **Movement**: Sometimes, the best way to dissipate emotional energy is through physical activity. A brisk walk, some gentle stretching, or a series of yoga poses can help release tension.

Building a Personal Toolkit

Just as a carpenter has a toolbox for different jobs, we need a personal toolkit for managing our emotions. This toolkit should be tailored to fit our unique needs and situations, filled with strategies that we know work for us.

- **Identify your go-to strategies**: Reflect on past instances when you were able to manage your emotions successfully. What did you do? Was it taking a walk, talking to a friend, or writing in a journal?
- **Experiment**: Be open to trying new techniques. What works for one person might not work for another, and what works in one situation may be less effective in another.

- **Accessibility:** Ensure your tools are easily accessible when you need them. If deep breathing helps, practice it regularly so it becomes second nature. If journaling is your outlet, carry a small notebook with you.
- **Support network:** Include trusted friends or family members in your toolkit. Sometimes, a listening ear or a word of encouragement is all it takes to see things from a different perspective.

As we navigate through life, the ability to regulate our emotions is a skill that benefits not only ourselves but also those around us. It fosters resilience, enhances our relationships, and enables us to face challenges with grace and composure. By identifying our emotional triggers, embracing the power of pause, employing strategies to calm our minds, and building a personal toolkit, we equip ourselves to navigate the seas of emotion with skill and confidence.

3.6 The Art of Self-Reflection: Journaling and Other Techniques

The act of self-reflection stands as a silent yet profound dialogue with oneself, a process where questions are posed, answers are sought, and insights emerge. This internal conversation is pivotal, allowing us to peel back the layers of our experiences, thoughts, and emotions to reveal the core of who we are and aspire to be. Among the myriad ways to engage in this self-dialogue, journaling emerges as a particularly potent method, offering a canvas upon which our inner narratives can unfold.

Journaling for Growth

Journaling, in its essence, is a practice of translating thoughts and feelings onto paper, a ritual of introspection that grants clarity and perspective. It serves multiple functions - as a repository for our deepest thoughts, a record of our growth, and a tool for emotional catharsis. When we journal:

- We gain clarity as the act of writing compels us to crystallize nebulous thoughts and feelings.
- We identify patterns in our behavior and responses, making it easier to recognize what triggers our emotions and why.
- We process emotions more healthily, using the page as a space to express feelings fully and freely.

To harness journaling effectively, consider these approaches:

- **Free Writing**: Set a timer for 5-10 minutes and write without pause or concern for grammar or structure. Focus on what feels most pressing or significant at the moment.
- **Prompted Journaling**: Use specific questions or prompts to explore different aspects of your emotional and mental landscape. For example, "What situation made me feel anxious today, and how did I respond?"

Structured Reflection Exercises

For those seeking more direction in their self-reflection, structured exercises can provide a framework that guides the exploration of one's inner world. These exercises are designed to probe deeper into our psyche, illuminating areas we might overlook or avoid. Some structured exercises include:

- **Gratitude Lists**: Regularly jot down things you're grateful for. This practice shifts focus to the positive, fostering a sense of contentment and well-being.
- **Emotion Deep Dive**: Select a single emotion you've experienced recently and dissect it. What prompted it? How did it manifest physically? What thoughts accompanied it?

Alternative Reflection Methods

While journaling is a powerful tool for many, it may not resonate with everyone. Fortunately, self-reflection is not confined to the written word. Various other methods can facilitate this introspective journey:

- **Verbal Reflection**: Speaking your thoughts aloud, whether to yourself, a voice recorder, or a trusted confidant, can offer a different path to clarity and understanding.
- **Creative Expression**: Drawing, painting, or crafting can serve as a non-verbal form of journaling, allowing emotions and thoughts to flow through your chosen medium.
- **Digital Platforms**: Apps designed for self-reflection offer prompts, tracking, and insights that can complement or serve as alternatives to traditional journaling.

Adopting one or a combination of these methods can enrich the self-reflection process, offering diverse avenues for exploring and understanding your inner world.

Regular Practice

The true power of self-reflection lies in its regular practice. Like any skill, its benefits are proportionate to the consistency and dedication with which it is pursued. Making self-reflection a daily or weekly habit ensures a continuous dialogue with oneself, fostering sustained growth and self-awareness. Consider setting aside a specific time each day or week for this practice, treating it with the same importance as any other appointment or commitment.

Regular self-reflection, regardless of the method chosen, acts as a compass, guiding us through the complexities of our internal landscapes. It allows us to navigate our emotions, behaviors, and thoughts with greater understanding and control. By dedicating time to this practice, we not only deepen our self-awareness but also enhance our capacity to live fully and authentically, aligned with our deepest values and aspirations.

3.7 Mindfulness Practices to Enhance Self-Awareness

Incorporating mindfulness into the rhythm of our daily lives transforms the mundane into moments of profound self-discovery. This subtle shift in approach can illuminate the hidden corners of our psyche, offering insights that guide us toward a deeper understanding of our thoughts, actions, and reactions. Mindfulness, then, is not merely a practice but a lens through which we view our existence, bringing into focus the nuances of our internal landscape.

Integrating Mindfulness into Daily Life

Embedding mindfulness into everyday routines begins with intention. It's the decision to be present, whether you're washing dishes or walking to work. Each task, no matter how small, becomes an opportunity to anchor yourself in the now. Here are some practical ways to weave mindfulness into the fabric of your day:

- **Start with a Mindful Morning:** Before the day's demands pull you into the current, take a few moments to ground yourself. Savor

your morning beverage, feel its warmth, and taste each sip. Let this act of mindfulness set the tone for your day.
- **Mindful Reminders:** Set random alarms or notifications on your phone as prompts to pause and breathe. Use these interruptions as cues to check in with yourself, observing your current emotional state and bodily sensations.
- **Turn Waiting into Mindfulness:** In moments of waiting — at the traffic light, in line at the grocery store, or before a meeting starts — resist the urge to reach for your phone. Instead, use this time to notice your breath, your surroundings, and the sensations in your body.

The Role of Meditation

Meditation sits at the heart of mindfulness, offering a structured method to cultivate this state of being. It teaches us to observe our thoughts without attachment, recognizing them as transient visitors in the vastness of our consciousness. For those new to meditation, starting can seem daunting, yet it's simpler than it appears:

- **Find a Quiet Space:** Choose a peaceful spot where you can sit undisturbed for a few minutes each day.
- **Start Small:** Begin with just 5 minutes of meditation daily. Gradually increase the duration as you become more comfortable with the practice.
- **Focus on Your Breath:** Use your breath as an anchor, bringing your attention back to it whenever your mind wanders.
- **Be Kind to Yourself:** The mind's tendency to wander is natural. When you notice your thoughts drifting, gently guide your focus back to your breath without self-criticism.

Mindful Eating and Movement

Mindful eating and movement bring awareness to the often automatic acts of consuming food and physical activity, transforming them into acts of mindfulness. Through these practices, we not only develop a deeper connection with our bodies but also enhance our appreciation for the nourishment and mobility they offer.

- **Mindful Eating:** Engage all your senses as you eat. Notice the colors, textures, and flavors of your food. Chew slowly, savoring each bite, and pay attention to your body's hunger and fullness cues.
- **Mindful Movement:** Whether you're exercising, stretching, or simply walking, focus on the sensation of movement in your body. Observe how your muscles feel, the rhythm of your breath, and the way your weight shifts with each step.

Using Mindfulness to Observe Thoughts

Our thoughts have a profound impact on our emotions and behaviors, yet they often go unexamined. Mindfulness offers a way to observe our thoughts with detachment, recognizing them as passing phenomena rather than definitive truths about ourselves or our lives.

- **Notice Your Thoughts:** Several times a day, pause to observe the flow of your thoughts. Imagine sitting by a river, watching your thoughts float by like leaves on the water's surface.
- **Label Thoughts:** As you observe your thoughts, gently label them. For example, "planning," "worrying," or "remembering." This practice helps in detaching from them, reducing their impact on your emotional state.
- **Shift Your Perspective:** When you become aware of negative or self-critical thoughts, consciously shift your perspective. Ask yourself, "Is this thought helpful? Is it true?" Often, you'll find that many thoughts lose their power when viewed through the lens of mindfulness.

Through these practices, mindfulness becomes more than a solitary act of meditation; it becomes a way of life. It infuses each moment with awareness, transforming routine actions into opportunities for self-discovery and growth. As we learn to integrate mindfulness into our daily lives, we open ourselves to a richer, more nuanced understanding of our inner world. Through meditation, mindful eating, movement, and the observation of our thoughts, we cultivate a state of being that is fully present and deeply connected to the essence of who we are.

3.8 Breaking the Cycle: Identifying Triggers and Creating New Responses

In navigating the complex waters of our emotional world, understanding what sparks our less-than-ideal reactions is paramount. It's akin to mapping out the terrain of a familiar yet unpredictable landscape — knowing where the landmines are buried enables us to tread more carefully or choose an entirely different path. This section will guide you in recognizing your personal emotional triggers that often lead to toxic behavior, understanding their origins, and crafting more constructive responses.

Identifying Personal Triggers

The first step in altering our reactive patterns is to pinpoint exactly what sets them off. Emotional triggers are deeply personal, varying widely from one individual to another. They can range from specific words and tones of voice to broader situations like feeling ignored or criticized. To identify your triggers:

- Reflect on recent instances where you felt overwhelmed by emotion. What was the common thread among these situations?
- Note the types of interactions, environments, or even times of day when you're most likely to react negatively. Is it during family gatherings, workplace meetings, or perhaps late at night when you're tired?

Understanding the Source of Triggers

Grasping the root cause of our triggers is crucial for effectively managing them. Often, these triggers are tied to past experiences, unresolved issues, or unmet needs. For instance, a trigger around feeling ignored might stem from childhood experiences of not feeling heard by caregivers. To delve into the origins of your triggers:

- Engage in reflective practices such as journaling or meditation to explore the memories and feelings associated with your triggers.
- Consider professional support, such as therapy, to help uncover and work through deeper, more complex sources of your triggers.

Creating New Response Patterns

Once you've identified and understood your triggers, the next step is to develop new, healthier ways of responding. This doesn't mean suppressing your emotions but rather allowing yourself to feel them fully while choosing a response that aligns with the person you want to be. Strategies include:

- Pause before reacting. Use this time to take a few deep breaths, grounding yourself in the present moment.
- Express your feelings using "I" statements. Instead of saying "You make me feel ignored," try "I feel upset when I don't feel heard."
- Plan for trigger scenarios. If you know certain situations are likely to set you off, prepare a response in advance. This could be a mental affirmation, a physical action like stepping away, or a phrase to express your feelings calmly.

The Role of Support in Changing Responses

Altering deeply ingrained response patterns is challenging and rarely a linear process. Support from trusted friends, family, or professionals can be invaluable. This support can take various forms:

- Sharing your goals with close ones can provide accountability and encouragement.
- Joining a support group or community where members share similar struggles can offer a sense of belonging and mutual understanding.
- Professional guidance, whether through therapy or coaching, can provide personalized strategies and insights to navigate your emotional landscape more effectively.

In crafting new responses to old triggers, the emphasis is on progress, not perfection. Each step forward, no matter how small, is a victory in the journey towards healthier emotional regulation and more fulfilling relationships.

3.9 Creating a Personal Accountability System

In the realm of self-improvement and the quest to shed toxic behaviors, accountability emerges as a silent guardian. It acts as a gentle but firm hand guiding us back on track when we stray. The beauty of accountability lies in its simplicity and its power to transform intention into action. This section will explore the significance of accountability, how to establish a personal accountability system, leverage technology in this endeavor, and the vital role of celebrating every step forward.

Accountability is not about self-surveillance or punitive measures. Instead, it's about creating an environment where our commitments to change are supported and nurtured. It's acknowledging that while the road to self-improvement is ours to walk, we don't have to do it alone. The presence of a checkpoint, be it a person or a system, serves as a reminder of our goals, providing both motivation and a framework to assess progress.

Setting up an Accountability System

Creating an effective accountability system begins with clear, achievable goals. These should be specific enough to guide your actions yet flexible enough to adapt as you grow. Here are steps to establish this system:

- **Identify Your Goals:** Write down what you wish to accomplish or the behaviors you want to change. Be as specific as possible.
- **Self-Check-Ins:** Schedule regular intervals—daily or weekly—to review your progress. This can be a quiet time of reflection or a structured review of your goals and actions.
- **Accountability Partners:** Choose someone you trust to be your accountability partner. This should be a person who can offer support without judgment, encouraging you to stay committed to your goals.

The synergy between self-check-ins and having an accountability partner creates a robust system. While self-check-ins promote independence and self-reflection, an accountability partner offers external support, motivation, and a different perspective.

Using Technology for Accountability

In today's digital age, technology stands as a steadfast ally in our accountability efforts. Numerous apps and online platforms are designed to track progress, set reminders, and even connect us with communities striving towards similar goals. Here's how you can integrate technology into your accountability system:

- **Goal-Tracking Apps**: Utilize apps that allow you to set, track, and share your progress towards your goals. Many of these apps also provide reminders and motivational quotes to keep you focused.
- **Online Communities**: Join forums or social media groups dedicated to self-improvement. These platforms offer a space to share experiences, challenges, and successes, fostering a sense of community and mutual support.

By integrating technology into your accountability system, you enhance your ability to stay committed to your goals, leveraging reminders, progress tracking, and community support to keep you motivated.

Celebrating Progress

One of the most crucial yet often overlooked aspects of accountability is celebrating progress. Recognizing and celebrating each achievement, no matter how small, is essential for maintaining motivation and commitment. It reinforces the value of your efforts and the positive changes you're making. Here are some ways to celebrate your progress:

- **Acknowledge Your Efforts**: Take a moment to acknowledge the work you've put in. Recognizing your own efforts is a form of self-respect and appreciation.
- **Share Your Successes**: Share your achievements with your accountability partner or support network. This allows you to celebrate together and encourages others on their journey.
- **Reward Yourself**: Set up a system where you reward yourself for milestones reached. This could be as simple as a relaxing evening off, a special treat, or an activity you enjoy.

Celebrating progress not only bolsters your spirits but also solidifies the habit changes you're making, embedding them deeper into your lifestyle.

In weaving accountability into the fabric of our self-improvement efforts, we create a structure that supports our growth, keeps us aligned with our goals, and reminds us of our capacity to change. By setting up a personal accountability system, leveraging technology, and celebrating our progress, we reinforce our commitment to shedding toxic behaviors and embracing healthier ones.

As we close this section, let us remember that accountability, in its essence, is about connection—connection to our goals, to those who support us, and to the version of ourselves we strive to become. It's a gentle reminder that every step taken towards self-improvement, no matter how small, is a step towards a more authentic and fulfilling life.

I WOULD LOVE TO HEAR FROM YOU

If you found value in this book, I kindly ask for your review and for you to share your experience with others. Please take a moment to leave a review on Amazon and share how this book has impacted your path to personal growth.
Your feedback not only helps me, but it also guides others in their journey towards change. It's through your support and reviews that my book is able to reach the hands of other readers.
Please take 60 seconds to kindly leave a review on Amazon.
If you reside outside of US, please use the link in your order.

All it takes is 60 seconds to make a difference!

4

REPAIRING AND BUILDING HEALTHY RELATIONSHIPS

Imagine trying to tune into your favorite radio station but only catching static and fragments of sound. It's frustrating, isn't it? Now, think of that static as the noise cluttering our ability to truly listen in conversations. Clearing that static and tuning in properly doesn't just mean we hear more accurately; it allows us to connect on a deeper level, transforming our interactions and relationships. This chapter zeroes in on the transformative power of active listening, a skill often overshadowed by our impulse to respond or solve problems immediately.

Active listening is about fully engaging with the speaker, understanding their message, and acknowledging their feelings without immediately jumping to a response or judgment. Once honed, it's a skill that can significantly deepen the bonds we share with others, leading to more meaningful and fulfilling relationships.

4.1 Listening to Understand, Not to Respond

The Essence of Active Listening

The core idea behind active listening is simple: listen to understand, not to reply. But in practice, it requires a shift from our usual conversational habits. It means focusing entirely on the speaker, absorbing what they're saying without planning your next comment. This kind of listening can reveal layers of meaning and emotion you might otherwise miss and is often what the speaker needs most — to be truly heard.

Barriers to Effective Listening

Several obstacles can hinder our ability to listen effectively:

- **Distractions:** Whether it's our phones, background noise, or our own wandering thoughts, distractions can pull our focus away from the speaker.
- **Preconceptions:** Entering a conversation with preconceived notions about what the other person is saying can filter out what we actually hear.
- **Emotional reactions:** Strong emotions, whether the topic or an unrelated event triggers them, can cloud our ability to listen with an open mind.

To overcome these barriers:

- Create a distraction-free environment when having meaningful conversations.
- Challenge your assumptions and stay open to new insights.
- Recognize and manage your emotional reactions by taking deep breaths or asking for a moment to process.

Practical Listening Exercises

To develop your active listening skills, try implementing these exercises into your daily interactions:

- **Paraphrasing:** After the speaker finishes a thought, try paraphrasing back to them what you've understood. This approach shows that you're listening and clarifies any misinterpretations.
- **Asking open-ended questions:** Questions that can't be answered with a simple yes or no prompt deeper conversation and show genuine interest in the speaker's thoughts.
- **Non-verbal cues:** Nodding, maintaining eye contact, and leaning forward slightly are all non-verbal ways to show the speaker you're engaged.

The Impact on Relationships

Active listening can revolutionize relationships in several ways:

- **Fosters deeper connections:** When people feel heard, they're more likely to open up, share more, and trust you with their thoughts and feelings.
- **Reduces conflicts:** Many arguments stem from misunderstandings that can be avoided with careful listening.
- **Strengthens emotional bonds:** Understanding each other on a deeper level strengthens the emotional bond between people, creating a more resilient relationship.

Incorporate active listening into your daily interactions, and watch your conversations and relationships transform. Whether with a partner, friend, colleague, or even a stranger, tuning into their words with your full attention can open up a world of deeper understanding and connection.

4.2 The Role of Honesty in Healing Relationships

In the intricate dance of human connection, honesty is the music that guides our steps, ensuring we move in harmony rather than stepping on each other's toes. Its role in mending and fortifying relationships cannot be overstated. Honesty isn't just about truth-telling; it's about creating an environment where transparency is the norm and vulnerability is met with understanding and respect.

The Importance of Transparency

Transparency in relationships is akin to opening the windows on a spring day, allowing fresh air to circulate and rejuvenate the space. It involves openly sharing our thoughts, feelings, and intentions, laying a foundation of trust that becomes the bedrock of healthy relationships. This openness fosters a deeper connection, as it invites our partners into our inner worlds, offering a full view rather than a sliver of who we are.

To cultivate transparency:

- Remember to share your thoughts and feelings regularly, not just when issues arise.

- Encourage your partner to share openly, showing appreciation for their honesty, regardless of the content.
- Discuss your hopes, fears, and dreams. Transparency is not just about the present but also about where you see your relationship going.

Navigating Difficult Truths

Sharing hard truths requires a delicate balance between honesty and compassion. It's about recognizing the weight of your words and their potential impact. The goal is not to avoid causing any discomfort—sometimes, growth stems from these uneasy spaces—but to ensure that the truth serves to build rather than break.

When sharing difficult truths:

- Choose a suitable time and place, ensuring you have privacy and won't be interrupted.
- Use "I" statements to express your perspective without placing blame, such as "I feel" or "I've noticed."
- Be prepared for a range of reactions and remain patient and supportive as your partner processes the information.

Building Trust Through Honesty

Trust grows in the fertile soil of honesty, nurtured by consistent truthfulness over time. It's about more than not lying; it's about being reliable, keeping promises, and showing up as your authentic self. Each act of honesty is a brick in the foundation of trust, and over time, a formidable structure is built, one that can weather the storms of doubt and insecurity.

Building trust requires:

- Consistency in your words and actions. Ensure that what you say matches what you do.
- Keeping promises, no matter how small they may seem. If you commit to something, follow through.
- Admitting when you're wrong. Owning up to mistakes is a powerful form of honesty that strengthens trust.

Honesty with Oneself

The journey toward fostering honesty in relationships begins with a commitment to self-honesty. It's a deep dive into our own motivations, fears, and desires, acknowledging our role in the dynamics and conflicts of our relationships. This inward honesty is sometimes the hardest to achieve, as it requires confronting aspects of ourselves we might rather ignore.

Cultivating self-honesty involves:

- Regular self-reflection. Take time to examine your thoughts, feelings, and behaviors critically.
- Acknowledging your flaws and mistakes. Recognize that imperfection is part of being human and that growth comes from facing our shortcomings.
- Seeking feedback from others. Sometimes, an external perspective can help us see truths about ourselves that we've missed or avoided.

In relationships, honesty is not just a policy but a practice that demands courage, compassion, and a commitment to growth. It's about creating a space where truths can be shared without fear, where transparency leads to trust, and where being our authentic selves is the highest form of intimacy. Through honesty, we heal and strengthen our relationships and pave the way for a deeper, more meaningful connection with those we love.

4.3 Navigating Difficult Conversations with Compassion

Difficult conversations are an inevitable part of human relationships, whether it's addressing a problem in a partnership, providing constructive feedback to a colleague, or discussing a sensitive issue with a friend. The mere anticipation of these discussions can evoke anxiety, but approaching them with compassion and preparation can transform potential conflicts into opportunities for strengthening bonds and understanding.

Preparing for Difficult Conversations

Before diving into a challenging dialogue, laying the groundwork internally is crucial. This preparation involves clarifying your intentions and envisioning the desired outcomes, which sets a constructive tone for the interaction. Here's how you can prepare:

- **Clarify Your Intentions:** Reflect on what you hope to achieve with the conversation. Is it to solve a problem, express your feelings, or understand the other person's perspective? Clear intentions guide your approach and help keep the discussion focused.
- **Anticipate Reactions:** Consider how the other person might react. Thinking through possible responses can help you prepare emotionally and strategize on how to keep the conversation productive.
- **Choose the Right Setting:** Select a time and place where both of you will feel comfortable and undistracted. Ensuring privacy and eliminating interruptions are key to fostering an open, honest dialogue.

The Role of Empathy

Empathy is the bridge that connects our experiences with those of others, allowing for a deeper understanding of their feelings and perspectives. Empathy softens the ground for mutual respect and understanding in difficult conversations, even when disagreements arise. To incorporate empathy:

- **Listen Actively:** Make a conscious effort to listen fully to the other person, seeking to understand their point of view without jumping to conclusions or planning your rebuttal.
- **Acknowledge Their Feelings:** Validating the other person's emotions shows that you respect their perspective, even if you don't agree. Simple acknowledgments like "I can see why you'd feel that way" can go a long way.
- **Be Curious:** Ask questions to deepen your understanding of their viewpoint. Approach these questions with genuine curiosity rather than as a tool to challenge or critique.

Practical Communication Techniques

Effective communication is the linchpin in navigating difficult conversations with grace. Employing compassionate communication techniques can prevent misunderstandings and foster a sense of mutual respect. Key techniques include:

- **Use "I" Statements:** Frame your sentiments from your perspective to avoid sounding accusatory. For example, "I feel upset when..." instead of "You make me feel upset by..."
- **Avoid Absolutes:** Phrases like "You always" or "You never" can make the other person feel defensive. Focus on specific behaviors or instances rather than generalizing.
- **Maintain a Calm Tone:** Your tone of voice can significantly impact how your message is received. Strive for calmness and clarity, even if the conversation becomes emotionally charged.

After the Conversation

The period following a difficult conversation is critical for healing and moving forward. Taking constructive steps can help ensure that both parties feel heard and that the dialogue leads to positive change.

- **Reflect on the Discussion:** Take some time to ponder the conversation. What did you learn about the other person's perspective? Did you convey your thoughts and feelings effectively?
- **Follow-up:** If appropriate, follow up with the other person. This could be a simple message expressing gratitude for the conversation or a more in-depth discussion about the next steps.
- **Take Action:** If you committed to making changes or taking certain actions during the conversation, follow through. Demonstrating your commitment to improvement can help rebuild trust and strengthen the relationship.

Navigating difficult conversations with compassion and preparation not only mitigates the potential for conflict but also paves the way for deeper understanding and connection. By approaching these discussions with empathy, employing effective communication techniques, and taking constructive steps afterward, we can transform challenging dialogues into catalysts for growth and strengthening bonds.

4.4 Setting and Respecting Boundaries in Relationships

Boundaries in relationships act like the guidelines on a highway, marking the paths that keep us safe and on course. They help define what is acceptable and what isn't, ensuring that everyone involved understands how to respect and value each other's space, feelings, and needs. The art of setting and respecting boundaries is crucial for the health and longevity of any relationship, whether familial, romantic, or professional.

Defining Personal Boundaries

At their core, personal boundaries are the limits we set for ourselves and others, encompassing our expectations, values, and principles. These boundaries can be emotional, indicating how we allow others to treat us, or physical, defining our personal space and touch preferences. Understanding and establishing these limits is the first step towards fostering respect and empathy within our relationships.

To identify your personal boundaries, consider the following steps:

- Reflect on past experiences where you felt discomfort, resentment, or anger due to someone's words or actions. These emotions often signal crossed boundaries.
- Determine your non-negotiables. What values, such as honesty, respect, or independence, are paramount to you?
- Evaluate your limits in various aspects of your life, including physical space, emotional sharing, and time management. What makes you feel safe and respected?

Communicating Boundaries Effectively

Once you have a clear understanding of your boundaries, the next step is to communicate them to others. Clear, assertive communication helps ensure that your boundaries are understood and respected without leaving room for ambiguity or misunderstanding.

To communicate your boundaries effectively:

- Be direct and specific. Instead of vague statements, clearly articulate your limits and expectations.
- Use assertive language that focuses on your needs and feelings. Phrases like "I feel" or "I need" can be effective in conveying your perspective.
- Choose an appropriate time and setting where you can discuss your boundaries without distractions or interruptions.

Remember, setting boundaries is not a one-time event but an ongoing process that might require adjustments as relationships evolve and grow.

Respecting Others' Boundaries

Just as we expect others to respect our boundaries, it's equally important for us to honor theirs. Respecting someone's boundaries is a testament to your regard for their feelings and well-being. It builds trust and deepens the connection, showing that you value the relationship and wish to maintain its health.

To respect others' boundaries, keep in mind the following guidelines:

- Listen actively when someone is communicating their boundaries to you. Acknowledge their needs and assure them of your respect for their limits.
- Pay attention to non-verbal cues. Sometimes, people may struggle to verbalize their boundaries, but their body language can offer clues about their comfort levels.
- If you're unsure about someone's boundaries, ask. It's better to seek clarification than to inadvertently cross a line.

Navigating Boundary Violations

Despite our best efforts, there may be times when boundaries are crossed, either by us or by someone else. How we handle these situations can significantly impact the resilience and quality of our relationships.

In cases of boundary violations:

- Address the issue promptly. Ignoring a boundary violation can lead to resentment and erode trust.
- Communicate your feelings and the specific boundary that was crossed. This conversation can be a learning opportunity for both parties.
- If you are the one who crossed a boundary, apologize sincerely and take steps to understand and respect the boundary in the future.

Setting and respecting boundaries are fundamental skills for any healthy relationship. They allow us to express our needs and values clearly while honoring those of others, creating a foundation of mutual respect and understanding. Through effective communication and ongoing vigilance in maintaining and adjusting these boundaries, we can build stronger, more fulfilling connections with the people in our lives.

4.5 The Art of Apologizing: Making Amends the Right Way

At the heart of mending and nurturing relationships, the act of apologizing plays a pivotal role. It's a gesture that goes beyond mere words to reflect a genuine recognition of wrongdoing and an earnest effort to set things right. A sincere apology can bridge gaps, heal wounds, and restore trust. Yet, not all apologies are created equal. The essence of a true apology lies in its components, the intention behind it, and the actions that follow.

The Components of a Sincere Apology

A genuine apology comprises several key elements, each serving a distinct purpose in the healing process:

- **Acknowledgment of Harm:** This involves clearly stating what you did wrong and acknowledging the impact of your actions on the other person. It's a step that validates their feelings and shows you understand the gravity of the situation.
- **Expression of Remorse:** Genuine remorse is crucial. It communicates that you regret your actions and their effect on the other person, showing empathy for their experience.
- **Commitment to Change:** A promise to avoid repeating harmful behavior in the future demonstrates your willingness to grow and improve. This commitment is a testament to the value you place on the relationship and your integrity.

These components lay the foundation for an apology that not only addresses the immediate hurt but also fosters long-term healing and growth in the relationship.

Going Beyond "I'm Sorry"

True amends extend far beyond the words "I'm sorry." They encompass actions and behaviors that demonstrate your commitment to rectification and change. Actions speak louder than words, and when it comes to apologies, they ring truer than any verbal expression of regret. To make amends effectively:

- **Make Restitution:** Whenever possible, take steps to rectify the harm caused. This could mean replacing something you broke, repaying a debt, or investing time and effort to help heal the emotional wounds.
- **Demonstrate Behavioral Change:** Actions that show you're working to alter your behavior in meaningful ways can reinforce your verbal apology and rebuild trust.
- **Offer Support:** Providing support to the aggrieved party in a way that respects their needs and boundaries can further demonstrate your sincerity and commitment to making things right.

Apologizing without Expectations

One of the most challenging aspects of apologizing is doing so without the expectation of forgiveness or reconciliation. True apologies are offered freely, without strings attached. They are an expression of your values and an acknowledgment of your responsibility, independent of the outcome. This approach respects the other person's autonomy and their right to process their feelings in their own time and way.

The Healing Power of Apologies

The impact of a sincere apology can be profound, both for the person offering it and the one receiving it. For the apologizer, it's an act of humility and courage that acknowledges their imperfections and their desire to do better. It's a step toward personal growth and self-improvement. For the recipient, a genuine apology can validate their feelings, begin the healing process, and sometimes pave the way for forgiveness and a stronger relationship.

Moreover, apologies have the power to transform the dynamics of a relationship by:

- **Restoring Dignity:** Apologies can help restore the dignity of the person who was wronged, acknowledging their worth and the injustice they experienced.
- **Building Empathy:** The process of apologizing fosters empathy, as it requires considering the feelings and perspective of the other person.
- **Strengthening Bonds:** By addressing past hurts and committing to

better behavior, apologies can strengthen the bonds between people, creating a foundation of trust and mutual respect.

Navigating the complexities of human relationships often involves making mistakes and inadvertently causing harm. The art of apologizing, when practiced with sincerity and depth, not only mends these rifts but also enriches our connections with others. It's a testament to the resilience of human relationships and the transformative power of humility, empathy, and the willingness to grow. Through acknowledging our faults, expressing genuine remorse, and taking concrete steps to make amends, we not only heal the wounds of the past but also lay the groundwork for healthier, more fulfilling relationships in the future.

4.6 Rebuilding Trust Through Consistent Actions

Trust sits at the core of every meaningful relationship, functioning as the glue that binds individuals together. Its presence fosters a sense of security and openness, allowing relationships to flourish. Conversely, the erosion of trust, often a consequence of toxic behavior, can destabilize even the strongest bonds. Repairing this foundational element demands a thoughtful approach, underscored by actions that consistently affirm one's commitment to change.

The process of restoring trust necessitates a multifaceted strategy, underscored by patience and a commitment to transparency. Here, we explore effective steps to mend the frayed ties and rebuild trust on a solid, more enduring foundation.

Steps to Rebuild Trust

Rebuilding trust is akin to nurturing a garden back to health—it requires time, effort, and the right conditions. The following steps provide a roadmap for those seeking to restore trust in their relationships:

- **Acknowledge the Breach:** Trust restoration begins with an honest acknowledgment of the actions that led to its erosion. This step is crucial for demonstrating awareness and taking responsibility for the impact of one's behavior.
- **Express a Genuine Apology:** A heartfelt apology can be a powerful healing catalyst. It should reflect an understanding of the

hurt caused, express genuine remorse, and convey a commitment to avoid repeating the harmful behavior.
- **Set Clear Intentions:** Articulate your intentions to rebuild trust and outline the specific actions you plan to take to achieve this goal. Sharing these intentions with the affected party can help set mutual expectations and provide a clear path forward.
- **Implement Consistent Behavior:** Consistency in actions and behavior is critical. Small, repeated actions that align with your expressed intentions can gradually restore confidence in your reliability and commitment.
- **Open Channels of Communication:** Maintain open, honest communication throughout the trust-building process. This includes regular check-ins to discuss progress, address concerns, and adjust actions as necessary.

The Role of Patience

Patience is an indispensable ally in the journey to rebuild trust. The process is inherently gradual, with progress often occurring in small increments. Recognizing that trust cannot be rushed is vital for setting realistic expectations and avoiding frustration. Patience affirms respect for the other person's feelings and their need for time to heal and regain confidence in the relationship.

Monitoring Progress and Setbacks

Monitoring the evolution of trust over time is crucial for understanding the effectiveness of your efforts and making necessary adjustments. The following strategies can aid in this monitoring:

- **Reflect Regularly:** Reflect on your actions and their impact on the relationship. Consider whether your behavior has been consistent with your intentions and the progress made in restoring trust.
- **Seek Feedback:** Encourage the other person to share their perspective on your efforts and the changes they've observed. This feedback can offer valuable insights into areas where additional work may be needed.
- **Acknowledge Setbacks:** Recognize that setbacks are a natural part of the process. When they occur, address them openly, explore their causes, and discuss strategies to prevent future occurrences.

Building trust is a complex, nuanced endeavor demanding unwavering commitment and transparency. Through consistent actions, patience, and open communication, it is possible to mend the fabric of trust and emerge with a stronger and more resilient relationship. The journey may be challenging, but the rewards—a relationship rooted in mutual respect, understanding, and trust—are immeasurable.

4.7 Cultivating Healthy Relationships: The Role of Mutual Respect

Mutual respect is the cornerstone upon which lasting, healthy relationships are built. It's the recognition and appreciation of each other's inherent worth, extending beyond mere tolerance to a deep understanding of and regard for each other's feelings, thoughts, and experiences. This mutual admiration fosters an environment where all individuals feel valued, heard, and empowered to express themselves freely.

Defining Mutual Respect

At its core, mutual respect in relationships means acknowledging each person's unique perspectives, values, and boundaries as valid and important. It's a commitment to interact with kindness and consideration, even when disagreements arise. This respect is evident in the way we speak to each other, how we respond to each other's needs and feelings, and in our willingness to compromise and negotiate to ensure everyone's well-being.

Respectful Communication

Maintaining respectful communication, especially during disagreements, is vital for sustaining healthy relationships. Here are strategies to ensure communication remains respectful:

- **Focus on the issue, not the person:** When discussing a problem, concentrate on the behavior or situation rather than making personal attacks. This approach helps to keep the conversation constructive.
- **Practice active listening:** Show respect by giving your full attention to the speaker, acknowledging their points, and responding thoughtfully.
- **Express yourself clearly and kindly:** Speak honestly about your feelings and needs using "I" statements, and avoid harsh language or criticisms.

- **Agree to disagree:** Recognize that it's okay to have differing opinions. Showing respect means valuing each other's viewpoints without needing to change them.

Recognizing and Addressing Disrespect

Recognizing signs of disrespect is crucial to addressing and resolving them constructively. Disrespect can manifest in various ways, including belittling comments, ignoring boundaries, or dismissive behavior. To address disrespect:

- **Identify the behavior:** Clearly identify which actions or words felt disrespectful.
- **Communicate your feelings:** Let the other person know how their behavior affected you, focusing on your feelings rather than accusing them.
- **Seek understanding:** Try to understand the intentions behind their actions. Sometimes, disrespect is not intentional and can stem from misunderstandings.
- **Request change:** Ask for specific changes in behavior that would make you feel more respected.

Building a Culture of Respect

Creating and maintaining a culture of respect within relationships requires continuous effort from all parties involved. It involves setting a positive example, reinforcing respectful behavior, and actively working to eliminate disrespect. Here are ways to cultivate a respectful environment:

- **Set mutual expectations:** Together, define what respect means in your relationship. Establish clear expectations for how you will treat each other and handle disagreements.
- **Lead by example:** Demonstrate respect in your actions and words. Your behavior sets a standard and encourages others to follow suit.
- **Celebrate differences:** Show appreciation for each other's unique qualities and perspectives. Recognizing and valuing diversity strengthens mutual respect.
- **Foster open dialogue:** Encourage open, honest communication. Create a safe space where everyone feels comfortable sharing their thoughts and feelings without fear of judgment.

Cultivating mutual respect is an ongoing process that enriches relationships, making them more fulfilling and resilient. It requires attentiveness, dedication, and a genuine desire to understand and value one another deeply. Through respectful communication, recognizing and addressing disrespect, and actively building a culture of respect, relationships can thrive, characterized by a profound appreciation for each other's individuality and a shared commitment to nurturing a positive, supportive environment.

4.8 Communication Skills for Conflict Resolution

In the tapestry of human relationships, conflict is a thread that, while often seen as a flaw, holds the potential to strengthen the fabric if woven with care. Recognizing conflict not as a harbinger of discord but as an opportunity for growth requires a shift in perspective. It's in the crucible of disagreement that our capacity for understanding, empathy, and connection can be forged and refined. This section explores the nuanced nature of conflict in relationships, offering strategies for resolution that not only resolve the immediate issue but enhance the relationship in the long run.

Understanding Conflict in Relationships

Conflict, at its core, arises from differences—differences in needs, desires, or perceptions. It's an inevitable part of any relationship, signaling not dysfunction but the presence of individuality within a partnership or group. The key lies in recognizing that the goal of addressing conflict isn't to emerge victorious but to reach a deeper understanding and find a solution that respects all parties involved.

To navigate conflict effectively, one must:

- Acknowledge the conflict early, resisting the urge to ignore it in hopes it will dissipate on its own.
- Approach the situation with an open mind, ready to explore all facets of the disagreement without preconceived notions.
- Recognize the shared goal of a stronger, healthier relationship as the foundation for any resolution strategy.

Conflict Resolution Strategies

Addressing conflict constructively opens a pathway to solutions that bolster the relationship. Implementing the following strategies can transform conflict from a source of tension to a catalyst for growth:

- **Create a Safe Space for Dialogue:** Begin by establishing an environment where all parties feel comfortable expressing their thoughts and feelings without fear of judgment or retaliation.
- **Practice Active Listening:** Commit to truly hearing each other's perspectives. This means listening not only for the content of what's being said but for the emotions and needs underlying the words.
- **Express Your Own Needs Clearly:** Use "I" statements to articulate your feelings and needs without placing blame. For instance, "I feel anxious when we don't discuss our plans in advance" rather than "You never tell me your plans."
- **Seek Common Ground and Compromise:** The heart of conflict resolution often lies in finding areas of agreement and compromise. This doesn't mean giving up your needs but rather exploring solutions that acknowledge and respect each person's perspectives and desires.
- **Employ Problem-Solving Techniques:** Together, brainstorm potential solutions, weighing the pros and cons of each. This collaborative approach leads to more creative solutions and reinforces the partnership.

Avoiding Common Pitfalls

Certain behaviors can exacerbate conflict, turning a manageable disagreement into a prolonged battle. Being aware of these pitfalls can help steer conversations toward constructive outcomes:

- **Steering Clear of Escalation:** Resist the impulse to raise your voice, interrupt, or use derogatory language. Escalation only heightens emotions and distances solutions.
- **Avoiding Assumptions and Generalizations:** Jumping to conclusions or using absolutes like "always" or "never" can derail productive dialogue. Focus on the specific issue at hand.

- **Resisting the Urge to Withdraw:** While taking a break can sometimes help cool down emotions, completely withdrawing from the conversation can signal disengagement and stall resolution.

Learning from Conflict

Every conflict carries lessons, offering insights into our own behaviors, the needs and desires of others, and the dynamics of our relationships. Reflecting on these lessons can deepen understanding and strengthen bonds:

- After resolving a conflict, reflect on what triggered the disagreement and how it was resolved. What worked well, and what could be improved?
- Consider the role that communication styles played in the conflict and resolution. Are there adjustments that could make future communication more effective?
- Use the resolution as a building block for your relationship. Implementing the agreed-upon solutions and changes demonstrates a commitment to the relationship and each other's well-being.

In navigating the complexities of conflict within relationships, we find opportunities for resolution and transformation. We can turn conflicts into stepping stones toward deeper connection and understanding by approaching disagreements with open hearts and minds, employing strategic communication tactics, and learning from each encounter. This approach helps fix and deepen relationships, showing how resilient and flexible our connections can be.

4.9 The Power of Vulnerability in Deepening Connections

In the realm of human connections, vulnerability is often seen through a lens of trepidation, mistakenly equated with weakness. However, it's this very openness, the willingness to expose our innermost selves, that acts as a catalyst for profound relationships. It's in the shared moments of vulnerability that bonds are fortified, trust is nurtured, and a deeper sense of intimacy is born.

The Strength in Vulnerability

At its core, vulnerability represents the courage to be seen for who we truly are, imperfections and all. It's the antithesis of weakness; it requires strength to lay bare one's fears, dreams, and insecurities. This act of bravery not only invites others to understand us on a more intimate level but also encourages them to reciprocate, fostering a mutual connection that is authentic and unguarded.

- **Vulnerability invites connection:** By sharing what lies beneath our surface, we invite others to connect with us on a deeper level.
- **It dismantles barriers:** Vulnerability has the power to break down the walls we erect around ourselves, allowing for genuine interactions that are not hindered by pretense or superficiality.

Sharing Vulnerabilities

Navigating the waters of vulnerability requires a careful approach, ensuring that we share our inner selves in a manner that fosters trust and safety. Here are guidelines to share vulnerabilities effectively:

- **Choose the right moment:** Timing is crucial. Look for moments of quiet intimacy where sharing will feel natural and be received with the attention it deserves.
- **Start small:** If the prospect feels daunting, begin with smaller admissions and gradually build up to more significant disclosures as trust deepens.
- **Be mindful of the recipient:** Consider the capacity of the other person to hold space for your vulnerabilities. Ensure they are someone who has shown empathy and understanding in the past.

Vulnerability and Intimacy

The link between vulnerability and intimacy is undeniable. Intimacy thrives on understanding and acceptance, qualities that are nurtured through the sharing of our inner worlds. As we reveal ourselves, we offer a map to our hearts and minds, inviting our partners to understand us in ways that surface-level interactions never could.

- **Deepens emotional intimacy:** Vulnerable exchanges promote a type of closeness that superficial conversations cannot achieve.
- **Enhances trust:** Each act of vulnerability strengthens the trust between individuals, laying a foundation for a relationship built on openness and authenticity.

Protecting Yourself When Vulnerable

While vulnerability is a path to deeper connection, it also necessitates a degree of caution to protect oneself emotionally. Here are strategies to ensure emotional safety while being vulnerable:

- **Assess the relationship:** Before opening up, evaluate the level of trust and respect present in the relationship. It's crucial to share vulnerabilities with those who have demonstrated they can handle them with care.
- **Set boundaries:** Be clear about what you are comfortable sharing and what areas you are not ready to open up about. It's okay to have limits.
- **Listen to your instincts:** Trust your gut feelings about when and with whom to share. If something feels off, it may be an indication to hold back.

In the landscape of human connections, vulnerability stands as a testament to our strength and capacity for depth. It challenges the misconception of vulnerability as a weakness, illuminating it instead as a profound source of strength that fosters deeper connections. By sharing our vulnerabilities in ways that are mindful and protective, we pave the way for relationships marked by trust, intimacy, and a profound understanding of one another. Through this openness, we not only allow ourselves to be truly seen but also invite others into our inner sanctum, creating bonds that are both resilient and deeply rooted in mutual respect and empathy.

4.10 Detoxifying Your Social Circle: Choosing Relationships Wisely

Navigating the waters of social connections with discernment is akin to tending a garden. Just as a gardener nurtures the plants that flourish and prunes those that drain resources without bearing fruit, so too must we assess our relationships, fostering those that enrich our lives and reevaluating those that deplete our emotional energy. This process, while challenging, is vital for cultivating a social circle that supports our well-being and growth.

Assessing Relationships

The first step in detoxifying your social circle involves taking a close, honest look at your current relationships to identify any toxic patterns or influences. This assessment can be likened to holding a mirror up to your interactions, reflecting on the dynamics present and how they impact your emotional state. Consider the following indicators of unhealthy relationships:

- **Consistent negativity:** If interactions leave you feeling drained, insecure, or unhappy, more often than not, it may signal a toxic dynamic.
- **Lack of support:** Relationships should be reciprocal. A lack of support or interest in your well-being is a red flag.
- **Boundary violations:** Repeated disrespect for your boundaries is indicative of a toxic relationship.

To conduct this assessment, you might:

- Make a list of the people you spend the most time with and note how you feel during and after interactions with each person.
- Reflect on any recurring conflicts or feelings of discomfort and their sources.

Creating a Positive Social Circle

Once you've assessed your relationships, the next step is actively cultivating a social circle that is positive, supportive, and enriching. This involves both seeking out new connections that align with your values and nurturing existing relationships that contribute to your well-being. Strategies for building a positive social circle include:

- **Engaging in activities that reflect your interests:** Join clubs, groups, or online communities where you can meet people with similar values and interests.

- **Being proactive in your interactions**: Don't wait for others to reach out. Initiate plans and show interest in getting to know people better.
- **Fostering open communication**: Share your thoughts, feelings, and experiences. Open communication can deepen connections and encourage reciprocity.

Setting Boundaries with Difficult People

Inevitably, you'll encounter individuals who, despite your best efforts, consistently engage in toxic behavior. Setting boundaries with these individuals is crucial for protecting your well-being. Effective boundary-setting involves:

- **Communicating your needs clearly**: Let the person know what specific behavior is unacceptable and how you expect to be treated.
- **Staying firm in your resolve**: It's essential to enforce the boundaries you set consistently. If a boundary is crossed, communicate the violation and the consequences.
- **Limiting exposure**: In some cases, reducing the amount of time you spend with or completely distancing yourself from a toxic individual may be necessary.

Remember, setting boundaries is not about changing the other person's behavior—that's beyond your control. It's about taking steps to ensure your well-being and respect in the relationship.

The Importance of Reciprocity

At the heart of healthy relationships lies the principle of reciprocity—the mutual exchange of support, understanding, and kindness. Reciprocity ensures that the give-and-take in relationships is balanced, fostering a sense of fairness and mutual respect. Here are ways to cultivate reciprocity in your relationships:

- **Practice active giving and receiving**: Be generous in offering your support to friends and open to receiving support when you need it. This cultivates a balanced dynamic.
- **Express appreciation**: Regularly acknowledge and thank those in

your social circle for their support and friendship. Gratitude reinforces positive behaviors and deepens bonds.
- **Check-in with yourself and others:** Periodically assess whether your relationships feel balanced. If you notice an imbalance, it may be time for a conversation about your needs and expectations.

Creating and maintaining a healthy social circle is an ongoing process that requires attention, effort, and, at times, difficult decisions. By assessing your relationships, nurturing positive connections, setting boundaries with difficult individuals, and fostering reciprocity, you can build a social environment that supports your emotional well-being and personal growth. This, in turn, becomes a foundation upon which you can thrive, bolstered by the strength and support of genuine, healthy relationships.

4.11 Creating a Supportive Environment for Growth

The spaces we inhabit and the company we keep play a significant role in shaping our behaviors, attitudes, and, ultimately, our growth. Much like a plant reaching toward the sunlight, we, too, gravitate toward environments that nourish our desire to evolve, shedding toxic habits in favor of healthier ones. Recognizing the profound influence of our surroundings, this section explores strategies for cultivating an environment conducive to personal growth and recovery from toxicity.

The Role of the Environment in Personal Growth

The environment, encompassing both our physical spaces and social circles, acts as a mirror reflecting back at us, reinforcing our beliefs, behaviors, and self-image. A cluttered, chaotic space, for instance, can exacerbate feelings of stress and disorganization, while a serene, organized environment can promote calmness and focus. Similarly, a social circle that normalizes negativity and toxic behavior can hinder our efforts to change, while one that embodies positivity and growth can uplift and inspire us.

To leverage the environment for personal growth:

- Curate your physical space to reflect the changes you wish to see within yourself. Incorporating elements that bring you peace, such as plants, art, or calming colors, can create a sanctuary that supports your well-being.

- Assess your social environment. Identify relationships that drain your energy or encourage negative patterns and consider ways to adjust these dynamics or distance yourself from toxicity.

Fostering Supportive Relationships

The journey towards growth is rarely a solitary one. Having allies who support our aspirations, challenge us constructively, and provide encouragement can significantly impact our ability to change. These relationships act as a safety net, catching us when we falter and cheering us on as we make strides.

To cultivate supportive relationships:

- Communicate your goals and needs. Openly sharing your aspirations with friends and family invites them to be part of your support system.
- Seek out mentors or individuals who embody the traits you aspire to develop. Their guidance, insight, and example can be invaluable resources.
- Reciprocate support. Fostering a culture of mutual growth and encouragement within your relationships creates a virtuous cycle that benefits everyone involved.

The Impact of Community

Beyond our immediate social circles, the broader community plays a crucial role in our personal development. Communities, whether based on shared interests, goals, or challenges, offer a sense of belonging, collective wisdom, and a broader perspective that can enrich our understanding and approach to growth.

To leverage the power of community:

- Engage with groups or organizations aligned with your growth goals. This could range from joining a local fitness group to participating in online forums focused on personal development.
- Contribute to the community. Sharing your experiences, challenges, and successes can help others on their path, reinforcing your learning and creating deep connections within the group.

- Embrace diversity within the community. Exposure to varied perspectives and approaches can broaden your horizons, encouraging innovative thinking and problem-solving.

Environmental Cues for Positive Habits

Our environment is peppered with cues that can either trigger toxic behaviors or encourage positive habits. Being mindful of these cues and intentionally shaping them to support our growth can make a significant difference in our day-to-day choices and actions.

To create environmental cues that promote positive habits:

- Arrange your physical space to make engaging in positive habits easier. For example, if you aim to read more, create a cozy reading nook that invites you to spend time with a book.
- Use visual reminders of your goals and values. Motivational quotes, goal boards, or symbols of your aspirations placed in your environment can serve as constant reminders of the path you've chosen.
- Minimize triggers for toxic behaviors. Identify elements in your environment that prompt negative habits and take steps to remove or alter them. This might involve setting boundaries around technology use or reorganizing your space to reduce clutter and stress.

Crafting an environment conducive to growth involves more than just physical rearrangement; it's about creating a space, both physically and socially, that echoes your aspirations for change. By surrounding ourselves with positivity, support, and reminders of our goals, we build a fertile ground for transformation. This supportive environment not only nurtures our personal development but also reinforces our journey away from toxicity, guiding us toward a more fulfilled and authentic existence.

4.12 Encouraging Healthy Interactions in Professional Settings

Navigating the intricacies of professional relationships requires a keen understanding that the workplace is a melting pot of diverse backgrounds, personalities, and communication styles. This diversity, while a source of strength, can sometimes give rise to toxic behaviors that undermine team cohesion and productivity. Recognizing the unique challenges of maintaining healthy interactions within professional settings is the first step toward fostering a positive work environment.

Professional Relationships and Toxicity

Toxic behaviors in the workplace can manifest in various forms, from overt harassment to subtler acts like exclusion or credit-grabbing. These actions not only damage individual well-being but can also erode the foundational trust necessary for team success. Identifying and addressing these behaviors promptly and effectively is crucial to maintaining a respectful and productive workplace.

Communication Strategies for Work

Clear, respectful communication is the backbone of effective teamwork and conflict resolution in professional settings. Employing targeted communication strategies can significantly enhance understanding and cooperation among colleagues. Tips for effective workplace communication include:

- Prioritizing clarity and conciseness to avoid misunderstandings.
- Using positive language, even when discussing challenges, to foster a constructive atmosphere.
- Encouraging an open exchange of ideas where all team members feel valued and heard.

Setting Professional Boundaries

Establishing and respecting personal boundaries within the workplace is vital for ensuring mutual respect and preventing burnout. Boundaries can relate to work-life balance, personal space, or the acceptable scope of professional responsibilities. Guidelines for setting healthy workplace boundaries include:

- Clearly defining your limits regarding work hours, task delegation, and personal space.
- Communicating your boundaries assertively yet respectfully to colleagues and supervisors.
- Respecting the boundaries of others, acknowledging that they may differ from your own.

Handling Conflict at Work

Conflicts, when managed constructively, can lead to growth and innovation. Therefore, developing strategies for effective conflict resolution is essential in any professional setting. Steps for managing workplace conflicts include:

- Addressing issues directly with the involved parties before escalating to higher management.
- Focusing on the problem at hand rather than personal attributes or past grievances.
- Striving for solutions that acknowledge and accommodate the needs and concerns of all parties.

In sum, creating a workplace environment that encourages healthy interactions requires a proactive approach to recognizing and mitigating toxic behaviors, employing clear and respectful communication, setting and honoring professional boundaries, and handling conflicts with a focus on collaborative solutions. These practices not only enhance individual well-being but also contribute to the overall success and productivity of the organization.

As we move forward, it's clear that the principles guiding our interactions in professional settings are not confined to the boundaries of the workplace. They echo the broader themes of respect, empathy, and accountability underpinning healthy relationships. In the next chapter, we'll explore how embracing these values in every aspect of our lives can lead to more fulfilling connections and a deeper sense of personal and collective well-being.

5

ADDRESSING COMMON CHALLENGES ON THE PATH TO TRANSFORMATION

Imagine a tree, steadfast in the wind, bending but not breaking. Its roots, deep and strong, anchor it against the storm. Similarly, our journey towards personal growth can face storms of criticism and doubt, both from within and from the world around us. The wind may howl, and the branches may shake, but like the tree, we have the strength to stand tall, rooted in self-belief and supported by our care network.

5.1 Dealing with Backlash: Navigating Criticism and Doubt

Criticism as a Tool for Growth

Criticism isn't always the enemy when it comes knocking on our door. It can be a mirror reflecting areas of ourselves we've overlooked. Imagine receiving feedback at work that your recent project fell short of expectations. It stings, right? But within that sting lies an opportunity. Take a step back and assess the feedback objectively: What can this teach me? Is there a grain of truth to it? Use it as a stepping stone to better your work and grow your skills.

Handling Doubt from Others

Doubt from others can feel like a weight, dragging down your spirits.

Picture this: you decide to quit smoking, but a friend quips, "I give it a week." That's doubt, loud and clear. Here's how you handle it:

- Smile and say, "I appreciate your input, but I am committed to this change. Let's talk about something else."
- Use their doubt as motivation. Prove them wrong, not through words but through action.
- Remember, their doubt doesn't define your capability. You do.

Building a Support System

A support system is your safety net. It's comprised of people who uplift you, believe in you, and are there when the going gets tough. Here's how to build yours:

- Identify who in your life makes you feel supported and valued. They're your go-to crew.
- Communicate openly with them about your goals and challenges. Let them know how they can support you.
- Reciprocate. Support is a two-way street. Be there for them as they are for you.

Criticism and doubt, whether from within or from others, are part of the process. They test our resolve but also offer us valuable lessons and opportunities for growth. By approaching criticism as a learning opportunity, handling doubt with grace, balancing feedback with self-trust, and cultivating a robust support system, you will navigate these challenges not as obstacles but as catalysts for transformation.

5.2 The Fear of Vulnerability and How to Overcome It

Embracing vulnerability can often feel like standing on a cliff's edge, with the vast unknown of potential reactions stretching out before us. It is a space where fear murmurs warnings of ridicule, misunderstanding, and rejection. However, it is also the very ground on which the magic of genuine connection and personal growth unfolds. The act of courage in being vulnerable isn't characterized by the lack of fear but rather by the ability to navigate and control it.

Identifying Fears

Before conquering the fear of vulnerability, we must first name it. This fear often stems from a variety of sources: past hurts that left scars, societal messages equating vulnerability with weakness, or even the dread of not being enough. Identifying these fears involves peeling back the layers of our experiences to understand the roots. Reflect on moments when the thought of opening up made you recoil. What were you afraid would happen? Pinpointing the source of your fear is the first step toward disarming it.

- Reflect on past instances when being open led to pain. How does this influence your current hesitance?
- Consider how societal norms and personal upbringing shape your views on vulnerability.
- Acknowledge the specific outcomes you fear, be it rejection, judgment, or loss of control.

Small Steps to Vulnerability

Confronting fear head-on doesn't mean leaping without a safety net. Start with small disclosures, choosing safe spaces and trusted people to share. It could be as simple as expressing a preference or sharing a memory. Each small step serves as a building block, gradually constructing a bridge over the chasm of fear toward a place of openness.

- Share a personal like or dislike in a casual conversation.
- Express an emotion related to a neutral topic, such as a movie or book.
- Confide in a trusted friend about a minor concern or fear.

The Role of Self-compassion

Self-compassion is the gentle hand that steadies us when the fear of vulnerability shakes our resolve. It reminds us that setbacks are not failures but part of the human experience. When a moment of openness doesn't go as hoped, wrap yourself in the same kindness you would offer a friend. Understand that courage lies not in the outcome but in the attempt.

- Practice self-kindness when feelings of vulnerability lead to discomfort. Remind yourself that it's brave to open up.
- Normalize setbacks as part of the growth process. Each experience provides valuable lessons for future attempts at vulnerability.
- Celebrate your courage in facing your fears, regardless of the immediate outcome.

Vulnerability as a Strength

Redefining vulnerability from a perceived weakness to a recognized strength shifts the entire narrative. It transforms vulnerability into a testament to our courage and confirms our commitment to authentic connections. Vulnerability opens doors to deeper relationships, fosters genuine self-expression, and catalyzes personal growth. In our most exposed moments, we often find our strongest connections, those built on mutual understanding and respect.

- Recognize moments of vulnerability as opportunities for growth and connection.
- Observe how vulnerability can lead to stronger, more authentic relationships.
- Acknowledge vulnerability as an act of bravery and a source of strength.

Facing the fear of vulnerability is a journey marked by introspection, small yet significant steps, self-compassion, and a reevaluation of vulnerability itself. It requires recognizing and naming our fears, taking incremental steps towards openness, wrapping ourselves in kindness when we stumble, and ultimately, viewing vulnerability as a conduit to strength. Through this process, we not only learn to navigate our fears but also unlock the door to a life rich with authentic connections and personal growth.

5.3 Staying Motivated During Difficult Times

Motivation, much like the ebb and flow of the ocean's tides, is subject to fluctuations. There are days when it washes over us in abundance, propelling us forward with ease. Then, there are periods when it recedes, leaving us stranded on the shores of stagnation and doubt. Recognizing that motivation's inconsistency is a natural part of the human experience can arm us with the strategies needed to navigate its low tides, ensuring we remain anchored in our commitment to personal transformation.

The Nature of Motivation

Understanding that motivation's intensity will vary allows us to anticipate and prepare for its inevitable dips. It's during these moments, when our drive starts to wane that our determination is truly tested. The key lies in maintaining a steady pace, reminding ourselves of the reasons behind our pursuit of change. Visual reminders, such as a written list of reasons or a vision board, can serve as tangible anchors to our initial spark of motivation, guiding us through periods of diminished drive.

- Reflect on why you started: Revisit your decision to change when motivation starts to dwindle.
- Visual reminders: Create a vision board or a list of goals and reasons for change that you can turn to for inspiration.

Setting Realistic Goals

Ambitious goals are commendable, yet they often come with the risk of overwhelming us, especially when motivation is low. Setting realistic, achievable goals acts as a safeguard against this, ensuring we can maintain progress without succumbing to discouragement. Break larger goals into smaller, manageable tasks, celebrating each completion as a step closer to the ultimate objective. This approach not only keeps motivation alive but also instills a sense of accomplishment that fuels further action.

- Break goals into smaller tasks: Divide larger objectives into achievable steps to prevent feeling overwhelmed.
- Celebrate small victories: Acknowledge and celebrate each completed task, no matter how minor it may seem.

Finding Inspiration

External sources of inspiration can reignite our motivation, pushing us beyond the confines of our comfort zones. Whether it's through the wisdom shared by mentors, the resilience depicted in literature, or the solidarity found within community groups, these external sparks can illuminate our path during times of darkness. Actively seek out stories of those who've navigated similar challenges, attend workshops or seminars, and engage with community groups aligned with your goals. The energy and determination of others can be contagious, rekindling your own drive to persevere.

- Seek mentorship: Connect with individuals who inspire you and can offer guidance and support.
- Engage with literature and media: Read books, watch documentaries, and listen to podcasts that motivate and educate.
- Join community groups: Surround yourself with like-minded individuals who can offer encouragement and understanding.

Celebrating Progress

The journey of personal transformation is marked by both its challenges and triumphs. Recognizing and celebrating every step of progress, however small, is vital for sustaining motivation. These moments of celebration act as milestones, reminding us of how far we've come and why we embarked on this path. Keep a journal of achievements, share your progress with supportive friends or family, or simply allow yourself a moment of gratitude for the courage to change. This practice not only bolsters motivation but also deepens our appreciation for the journey itself.

- Journal your achievements: Keep a record of your progress and reflect on it during moments of low motivation.
- Share your journey: Discuss your achievements with supportive individuals who can celebrate with you.
- Practice gratitude: Take time to be thankful for the progress made, acknowledging the effort and determination it required.

Navigating through the ebbs and flows of motivation requires an understanding of its nature, the setting of realistic goals, seeking external inspiration, and a commitment to celebrating every step of progress. By embracing these strategies, we equip ourselves with the tools needed to maintain momentum, even during the most challenging times. It's through persistence, resilience, and a celebration of the journey's every milestone that we find the strength to continue moving forward, motivated by the promise of transformation and the endless possibilities that lie ahead.

5.4 Handling Relapses: What to Do When You Slip Up

In the dance of personal transformation, missteps are inevitable. Picture a relapse not as a fall from grace but as a misstep in a complex choreography. It's a part of the dance, not the end of the performance. Removing the stigma from these slips, understanding their triggers, crafting a plan for future incidents, and embracing self-forgiveness pave the way for a graceful recovery and continued progress.

Normalizing Relapses

In the context of personal growth, a relapse can evoke feelings of failure. However, it's crucial to recognize these moments as a natural aspect of the change process and use them as learning opportunities. Acknowledging them as part of the journey demystifies setbacks, making them less daunting and more manageable. Remember, even the most seasoned professionals in any field understand that perfection is a myth; growth is non-linear, marked by peaks and valleys.

- Accept relapses as part of the growth process, not indicators of failure.
- Shift the narrative around relapses from setbacks to stepping stones for learning.

Learning from Relapses

Each relapse carries valuable lessons. By examining the circumstances leading up to it, we can uncover patterns and triggers that may not have been apparent before. This introspection enables us to fortify our strategies against future vulnerabilities. For instance, if stress at work leads you to revert to a toxic habit, recognizing this trigger is the first step towards developing healthier coping mechanisms.

- Reflect on the situation or emotions that preceded the relapse.
- Identify patterns or common triggers that may contribute to relapses.

Creating a Relapse Plan

Forearmed is forewarned. A relapse plan is a proactive strategy designed to navigate through and out of a setback. It outlines steps to take when you notice warning signs, ensuring that a lapse doesn't turn into a full-blown relapse. The plan could include reaching out to a supportive friend, engaging in a particular self-care activity, or practicing mindfulness to center yourself.

- List early warning signs that indicate a potential relapse.
- Outline specific, actionable steps to take when you notice these signs.
- Identify supportive individuals you can reach out to in moments of vulnerability.

Self-forgiveness and Moving Forward

Perhaps the most critical aspect of handling relapses is self-forgiveness. Harboring guilt or self-blame serves only to perpetuate the cycle of negative behavior. Instead, offer yourself the same compassion and understanding you would extend to a friend in a similar situation. Recognize your efforts, acknowledge the difficulty of your chosen path, and reaffirm your commitment to your goals. This mindset facilitates recovery from relapses and strengthens your resilience, empowering you to move forward with renewed vigor.

- Practice self-compassion. Acknowledge the effort and courage it takes to pursue personal growth.
- Understand that perfection is unattainable and that setbacks do not define your worth or your journey.
- Reaffirm your commitment to your goals, recognizing that each step, forward or backward, is part of the progress.

In navigating the path of personal transformation, relapses are not roadblocks but rather detours offering insights and opportunities for deeper self-awareness and growth. By normalizing these experiences, learning from them, preparing for their eventuality, and practicing self-forgiveness, we equip ourselves with the tools necessary for a resilient and enduring commitment to our personal development goals. It's in the dance of advancing, retreating, and advancing again that we find our rhythm and our way forward.

5.5 The Importance of Patience and Perseverance

In the realms of personal transformation, patience is not merely a virtue but a necessity. Recognizing that real change unfolds over time allows us to set a pace that acknowledges progress and respects the process. This understanding lays the groundwork for building perseverance, a quality that ensures we remain steadfast in our pursuit, even when immediate results seem elusive.

The Role of Patience

Patience teaches us to appreciate the journey, understanding that each step, no matter how small, is a move in the right direction. It's about allowing ourselves the space to grow at our own pace, free from the pressure of unrealistic expectations.

- **View each day as an opportunity:** Instead of focusing on the end goal, see every day as a chance to implement small changes and learn.
- **Embrace the learning process:** Understand that setbacks are not failures but lessons that provide insights into what works and what doesn't.

Patience is the calm acceptance that things can happen in a different order than the one you had in mind. It's about maintaining your composure and optimism, even when progress seems slow.

Building Perseverance

Perseverance, the steadfast effort to follow through on a commitment despite difficulties, is cultivated by focusing on the larger picture while celebrating smaller achievements along the way.

- **Anchor in your vision:** Keep your long-term vision in sight. It serves as a reminder of why you started and where you intend to go.
- **Set achievable milestones:** Breaking down your goal into smaller, achievable milestones makes the journey more manageable and less daunting.
- **Practice mindfulness:** Engage in mindfulness to stay present and

reduce feelings of overwhelm. It helps in appreciating the current moment and the progress being made.

Perseverance is fueled by an unwavering belief in oneself and the conviction that the destination is worth the trials encountered on the journey.

Dealing with Frustration

Frustration is an inevitable companion on the road to change, often arising from unmet expectations or perceived stagnation. Managing frustration effectively is crucial in maintaining motivation and perseverance.

- **Reframe your perspective:** When frustration sets in, try to reframe your perspective. Look for the silver lining in setbacks and view them as opportunities for growth.
- **Break tasks into smaller steps:** If a goal feels overwhelming, break it into smaller, more manageable tasks. This makes it easier to tackle and reduces feelings of frustration.
- **Engage in self-care:** Prioritize self-care to manage stress and recharge your emotional batteries. Activities like exercise, reading, or spending time in nature can provide a much-needed break and shift in focus.

Frustration, when managed well, can transform from a roadblock into a catalyst for renewed effort and creativity.

Celebrating Endurance

The act of perseverance itself deserves recognition. Celebrating the strength it takes to continue striving towards your goals reaffirms your commitment and bolsters your resolve. It's a recognition of the courage it takes to persist, especially when the path is steep.

- **Acknowledge your resilience:** Take time to reflect on the challenges you've overcome. Recognizing your resilience in the face of adversity fosters a sense of achievement and strength.
- **Share your journey:** Sharing the story of your journey with others can not only provide encouragement to those who might be struggling but also remind you of how far you've come.
- **Reward your perseverance:** Reward yourself for the perseverance shown. Whether it's treating yourself to something special or

simply taking a moment to bask in your own tenacity, acknowledging your effort is crucial.

The celebration of endurance is a powerful reminder of our capacity to withstand challenges, adapt, and emerge stronger. It is in recognizing the beauty of the struggle and the growth it brings that we find the strength to keep moving forward, armed with patience and perseverance, toward the realization of our fullest potential.

In this landscape of change, patience, and perseverance are our guides, teaching us to embrace each step, manage frustration with grace, and celebrate the strength it takes to persist. It is through these qualities that we navigate the complexities of transformation, making peace with the pace of progress and finding joy in the journey itself. With patience as our compass and perseverance as our drive, we continue to push forward, unwavering in our quest for personal growth and the fulfillment of our deepest aspirations.

5.6 Finding Joy in the Journey of Self-Improvement

The process of self-improvement often draws a picture of relentless effort and unwavering discipline, a path strewn with obstacles to overcome and goals to achieve. Yet, hidden within this narrative lies an opportunity to infuse our days with joy and discovery, transforming what might seem like a relentless march into a dance of exploration and pleasure. Here, we explore avenues to weave joy into the fabric of our self-improvement efforts, ensuring that each step forward is not only towards growth but also towards happiness.

Reframing the Journey

Imagine for a moment viewing your path to self-improvement not as a steep ascent up a mountain but as a stroll through a vibrant marketplace, each step offering a new sight, a new sound, a new taste. Such a shift in perspective opens us up to the richness of the experience, where every attempt, every lesson, and every moment of growth enriches our journey with depth and color.

- **View setbacks as detours:** Instead of seeing setbacks as blockades,

consider them detours that lead you through unexplored territories, each with its own lessons and insights.
- **Celebrate the process:** Focus on the excitement of learning and growing rather than just the end goals. This makes the journey enjoyable in itself, not just a means to an end.

Incorporating Joy

Sprinkling moments of joy throughout the process of self-improvement can dramatically alter our experience, making our pursuit not just sustainable but also delightful.

- **Integrate your passions:** Find ways to incorporate activities you love into your growth efforts. Love painting? Use it to explore and express your journey. Adore the outdoors? Make nature walks a time for reflection and goal setting.
- **Make it social:** Share parts of your journey with friends or family. Joining a class, forming a small group to share progress, or even just having a buddy can add a layer of enjoyment and accountability.

Mindfulness and Gratitude

Mindfulness and gratitude invite us to pause, to breathe, and to fully immerse ourselves in the present moment, appreciating the journey for what it is—a series of nows, each holding its own beauty and worth.

- **Practicing mindfulness:** By engaging in mindfulness techniques, such as meditation or pausing to fully absorb your environment, you anchor yourself in the present moment. This practice enables you to discover happiness within the journey itself, enriching your experience and appreciation of the now.
- **Cultivating gratitude:** Regularly acknowledge and express gratitude for your progress, however small. Keep a gratitude journal or share your thanks with someone who has supported you. This practice highlights the positive aspects of your journey, fostering joy.

The Balance Between Effort and Ease

Striking a balance between the effort required for change and moments of ease and relaxation is crucial. It ensures that our pursuit of self-improvement is not at the expense of our well-being but rather in harmony with it.

- **Listen to your body and mind:** Pay attention to signs of fatigue or stress and allow yourself the time to rest and recuperate. This might mean taking a day off your routine, indulging in a hobby, or simply doing nothing.
- **Integrate relaxation into your routine:** Make relaxation and ease an integral part of your daily routine. This could be through practices like yoga, reading for leisure, or engaging in any activity that brings you peace and relaxation.

In weaving joy into the journey of self-improvement, we not only enhance our daily experience but also reinforce our commitment to growth. By reframing our perspective, integrating moments of pleasure, practicing mindfulness and gratitude, and balancing effort with ease, we ensure that our path is not just one of achievement but also of happiness and fulfillment.

5.7 Navigating Loneliness and Isolation on Your Path

In the quest for self-improvement, moments of solitude can be both a sanctuary and a challenge. While solitude offers a space for introspection and personal growth, prolonged isolation can become a barrier, leading to feelings of loneliness and disconnection. Recognizing the fine line between these two states is crucial in ensuring that our time alone serves as a catalyst for development rather than a source of emotional distress.

The Role of Solitude

Solitude, when embraced, provides an invaluable opportunity for deep reflection and self-discovery. It's in these quiet moments that we can turn inward, examining our thoughts, motivations, and the progress we've made on our path. Solitude allows for a level of introspection that is often unattainable amidst the noise and distractions of daily life. To harness the benefits of solitude:

- Schedule regular periods of solitude into your routine, viewing them as appointments with yourself that are non-negotiable.
- Use solitude as a time for meditation, journaling, or engaging in any solitary activity that fosters self-awareness and reflection.
- Approach solitude with intention, setting goals for what you hope to achieve during these times, be it clarity on a specific issue or simply a moment of peace and relaxation.

Dealing with Loneliness

While solitude can be enriching, loneliness is its shadow, marked by feelings of isolation and disconnection. It's not uncommon to experience loneliness as we distance ourselves from toxic behaviors or relationships that no longer serve our growth. To navigate these feelings:

- Recognize that loneliness is a natural emotional response, not a reflection of your worth or social capabilities.
- Reach out to friends or family members, even if it's just for a casual chat. Sometimes, a simple conversation can alleviate feelings of isolation.
- Engage in activities that connect you with others, such as volunteering, joining clubs or classes that align with your interests, or attending community events.

Creating New Connections

As we shed old habits and relationships that hinder our growth, the importance of forging new, healthy connections becomes evident. Surrounding ourselves with individuals who support and inspire us can dramatically impact our well-being and progress. To cultivate these new connections:

- Be proactive in seeking out individuals or groups who share your values and goals. This could mean joining online forums, community groups, or local clubs that resonate with your interests.
- Take the initiative to introduce yourself and engage in conversations. While this may feel daunting, remember that many others are also looking to make new connections.
- Be open and authentic in your interactions. Genuine connections are built on honesty and vulnerability.

The Importance of Community

Finding or creating a community that aligns with your values and supports your growth is invaluable on the path to self-improvement. A community offers not just companionship but also motivation, inspiration, and a sense of belonging. In the presence of a supportive community, feelings of isolation are replaced with a sense of being understood and valued. To find your community:

- Explore local or online groups that focus on areas relevant to your journey, whether it's personal development, a specific hobby, or a cause you're passionate about.
- Attend workshops, seminars, or social events that are likely to attract like-minded individuals. These can be excellent opportunities to connect with others who share your interests.
- Consider starting your own group if you can't find one that meets your needs. This could be as simple as a book club, a walking group, or an online forum dedicated to a specific topic.

In traversing the path of self-improvement, understanding and balancing the roles of solitude and loneliness is essential. Embracing solitude for its potential to foster introspection and growth while actively navigating and addressing feelings of loneliness ensures that our journey is marked not by isolation but by meaningful connections and a strong sense of community. By creating new connections and immersing ourselves in supportive communities, we not only enrich our own lives but also contribute to the well-being and growth of those around us.

5.8 Self-Care as a Tool for Overcoming Challenges

Self-care, often misconstrued as indulgence or selfishness, truly stands as a foundational practice for sustaining our well-being through the ups and downs of personal change. It's a multifaceted approach to nurturing ourselves, ensuring we're in the best position to tackle the challenges that come with growth. The essence of self-care lies in its adaptability; it's not a one-size-fits-all but rather a personalized set of practices that resonate with and rejuvenate the individual.

Defining Self-Care

At its core, self-care embodies any action we consciously undertake with the intention of enhancing our physical, mental, and emotional health. From the simplicity of a nightly skincare routine to the commitment of regular exercise or the mental decluttering provided by journaling, self-care encompasses a broad spectrum of activities that support our well-being. It's the acknowledgment that our resources—energy, patience, resilience—are finite and need replenishing.

Personalizing Your Self-Care Routine

The beauty of self-care lies in its customization. What serves as a profound source of rejuvenation for one might not hold the same value for another. This personalization requires a deep understanding of oneself. To craft your self-care routine:

- **Identify what truly relaxes and rejuvenates you:** Reflect on activities that leave you feeling refreshed and invigorated. It could be as active as hiking through nature or as calm as reading by a window.
- **Consider your daily schedule:** Integrate self-care practices in a way that complements your routine rather than complicating it. A 5-minute meditation might fit better than an hour-long session for someone with a packed schedule.
- **Experiment and adjust:** Be open to trying new self-care practices and adjusting existing ones. Flexibility allows your self-care routine to evolve with your changing needs and preferences.

Self-Care and Resilience

The consistent application of self-care practices fortifies our resilience, equipping us with the strength to face and overcome obstacles. Like a river steadily carving its path through rock, regular self-care gradually builds a deep reservoir of resilience. This resilience enables us to navigate the tumultuous waters of change with grace and perseverance. To integrate self-care into building resilience:

- **Regularly schedule self-care:** Make it as non-negotiable as any important appointment. Consistency is key to building and maintaining resilience.

- **Use self-care as a stress management tool:** Recognize the signs of stress and have a go-to set of self-care practices to alleviate it. This proactive approach can prevent burnout and maintain your resilience through stressful periods.
- **Reflect on your resilience journey:** After periods of challenge, take time to reflect on how your self-care practices supported you. This reflection can reinforce the importance of self-care in building resilience.

Balancing Self-Improvement with Self-Compassion

In the pursuit of self-improvement, it's crucial to remember that being overly critical or pushing ourselves too hard can be counterproductive. Self-care serves as a reminder to balance ambition with kindness. This balance ensures that our efforts towards growth are sustainable and rooted in a healthy self-regard. Strategies for maintaining this balance include:

- **Set realistic goals:** Aim for progress, not perfection. Acknowledge your efforts and celebrate the small victories along the way.
- **Listen to your body and mind:** Pay attention to signs of fatigue or stress. Allowing yourself time to rest and recharge is not a setback but a vital component of sustainable growth.
- **Practice self-compassion:** Speak to yourself with kindness and understanding, especially during moments of struggle or failure. Remind yourself that growth is a process with its own ebb and flow.

In this approach to self-care as a tool for overcoming challenges, the emphasis is on the understanding that caring for ourselves is not a luxury but a necessity. It's the fuel that powers our journey of change, the quiet strength that sustains us through the trials of transformation. Through personalized routines, we not only maintain our well-being but also build the resilience necessary to navigate the complexities of personal growth. By balancing our drive for self-improvement with compassionate regard for our own well-being, we ensure that our journey is not only about reaching a destination but also about nurturing our health and happiness along the way.

5.9 Embracing Change as a Constant in the Journey of Growth

In the grand tapestry of life, change weaves its thread through every aspect, reminding us of the only true constant. Embracing this inevitability allows us to flow with life's currents rather than resist them, making our journey of self-improvement a dynamic and adaptive process. It's in this fluid dance with change that we find our true capacity for growth and transformation.

Adapting to change requires a blend of flexibility and openness, qualities that enable us to see the potential in the new and unfamiliar. Strategies for cultivating this adaptability include:

- **Stay curious:** Approach changes with a sense of curiosity rather than apprehension. This mindset can transform challenges into opportunities for learning and growth.
- **Build a flexible routine:** While routines provide structure, incorporating flexibility allows you to adapt to unexpected changes without feeling overwhelmed.
- **Cultivate a support network:** Surround yourself with people who embrace change positively. Their perspectives and experiences can inspire and guide you through your transitions.

The way we mentally prepare for and perceive change plays a pivotal role in shaping our experiences throughout the process. Viewing change as an opportunity rather than a threat opens us up to the possibilities that lie within the new and unknown. It encourages us to:

- **Challenge our comfort zones:** Stepping into unfamiliar territory can be daunting but also incredibly rewarding. It's here, in the discomfort of the unknown, that we discover new strengths and capabilities.
- **Learn from every experience:** Each change, regardless of its outcome, holds valuable lessons. Reflecting on these experiences enhances our understanding and fosters personal growth.
- **Remain open to evolving goals:** As we change, so too do our aspirations and dreams. Being open to this evolution ensures that our goals always align with our most authentic selves.

In navigating the constant flux of life, our ability to embrace change with grace and optimism is a powerful catalyst for growth. It enables us to ride the waves of transformation with resilience, continuously evolving and expanding the horizons of our potential. Through this embrace of change, we not only adapt to the shifting landscapes of our lives but also actively shape the journey of our becoming, ever forward, ever upward.

5.10 Embracing Change as a Constant in the Growth Process

Change, ever-present and inevitable, shapes the contours of our lives, sculpting our experiences and ourselves in its relentless progression. It's a force that, when accepted, propels us forward, molding us into more resilient, adaptable beings. Recognizing change as an inherent aspect of existence allows us to navigate its currents with less resistance and more grace.

Welcoming Change with Open Arms

The first step in making peace with change is acknowledging its constant presence. Life, in its essence, is dynamic, a series of transitions from one state to another. Welcoming change rather than bracing against it can transform our experience of life's unpredictability from one of apprehension to one of anticipation for the growth opportunities it presents.

- Accept change as a natural part of growth, understanding that it is through change that we evolve.
- View each new shift as a chance to learn and adapt, an invitation to expand your understanding of yourself and the world around you.

Flexibility and Openness: Keys to Adaptation

Adapting to change requires a degree of flexibility and a willingness to bend without breaking under the weight of new circumstances. This flexibility, coupled with an openness to the unfamiliar, equips us with the tools to navigate life's changes with poise.

- Cultivate flexibility by challenging your routines and allowing for spontaneity in your daily life. This practice can help prepare you for larger, unforeseen changes.

- Approach the unfamiliar with curiosity rather than fear. Ask questions, seek to understand, and be willing to explore new perspectives and possibilities.

Cultivating a Growth Mindset

How we perceive and react to change is significantly influenced by our mindset. A growth mindset, one that thrives on challenge and sees failure not as evidence of unintelligence but as a heartening springboard for growth and for stretching our existing abilities, can make all the difference.

- Foster a growth mindset by celebrating effort over success. Recognize that effort is a true measure of courage.
- Reframe challenges as opportunities. Instead of saying, "I can't do this," ask, "What can I learn from this experience?"
- Embrace failures as lessons. Every setback is a chance to gather insights and come back stronger.

Celebrating Your Evolution

Every shift, every transition, and every change brings us closer to the person we aspire to be. Celebrating this evolution is not just about acknowledging the milestones but also honoring the subtle shifts in our thoughts, behaviors, and perspectives that occur along the way.

- Take time to reflect on how you have changed over time. Acknowledge the growth, no matter how small it seems.
- Share your evolution with others. Your growth can inspire and motivate those around you.
- Recognize that change is proof of your commitment to growth. Celebrate the journey as much as the destination.

In a world that never stands still, embracing change as a constant companion on our path to growth allows us to navigate life's shifts with resilience and optimism. By welcoming change, remaining flexible and open, nurturing a growth mindset, and celebrating our evolution, we equip ourselves to ride the waves of transformation with assurance and poise. This approach not only makes the journey more manageable but also enriches our experience, turning the inevitable upheavals of life into opportunities for profound personal development.

As we close this chapter, it's clear that change, with all its unpredictability and potential for discomfort, is also a powerful catalyst for personal growth. By embracing it, adapting with flexibility and openness, and viewing it through the lens of a growth mindset, we transform our experience of change from something to be endured to something to be celebrated. This perspective not only prepares us for the inevitable shifts life throws our way but also allows us to see each change as a stepping stone, bringing us ever closer to our true potential. As we move forward, let us carry with us the lessons learned from these shifts and transitions, using them as a foundation for the continued journey of self-discovery and improvement that lies ahead.

6

BUILDING A FUTURE FREE FROM TOXICITY

Imagine you're repainting a room. The walls, once a dull, uninspiring beige, are ready for a transformation. You've chosen a vibrant color that sparks joy every time you imagine it on your walls. The process isn't just about covering the old with the new; it's about preparing the surface, filling in the cracks, and carefully applying each coat, knowing that the outcome will be worth the effort. This is much like cultivating a positive mindset; it's not about slapping a cheerful hue over the old thinking patterns but about transforming your mental landscape, layer by layer, into one that supports and sustains change.

6.1 Cultivating a Positive Mindset for Lasting Change

The Power of Positive Thinking

A positive mindset doesn't mean ignoring life's challenges but facing them confidently, expecting a good outcome. It's like wearing a raincoat during a storm; the raincoat doesn't stop the rain but can keep you dry and comfortable.

- **Science backs this up:** Studies have shown that positive thinking can lead to better stress management, improved health, and higher levels of achievement.

- **Start small:** Begin your day by identifying one thing you're grateful for. This could be as simple as a warm cup of coffee or a text from a friend. This act of recognition shifts your focus from what's lacking to what's abundant in your life.

Reframing Setbacks

Not every attempt at change will be smooth. When you hit a snag, think of it as a detour rather than a roadblock.

- **Find the lesson:** Ask, "What can I learn from this setback?" It could be a new strategy for handling stress or realizing what you truly value.
- **Change your self-talk:** Instead of saying, "I failed," try, "I found a way that didn't work, and that's okay."

Nurturing Optimism

Optimism isn't about expecting life to be easy; it's about trusting that you have what it takes to handle life's ups and downs.

- **Visual reminders:** Keep a note on your fridge or bathroom mirror with an uplifting quote or affirmation. Seeing this daily can help steer your thoughts in a positive direction.
- **Limit exposure to negativity:** This might mean setting boundaries around how much news you consume or spending less time with people who drain your energy.

Guarding Against Negativity

Negativity can come from external sources or from within. Protecting your mindset is crucial for sustaining positivity through the transformation process.

- **Mindful consumption:** Pay attention to how certain types of media or conversations affect your mood. Choosing uplifting content and discussions can help maintain a positive outlook.
- **Build a positivity circle:** Surround yourself with people who uplift and encourage you. Their support can act as a buffer against negativity.

Cultivating a positive mindset is like tending a garden. It requires regular care, the right nutrients, and a bit of sunshine. With each positive thought, you're planting a seed for future success, resilience, and happiness. Just as a garden doesn't bloom overnight, transforming your mindset is a gradual process, one that unfolds with each small, deliberate action.

6.2 The Role of Routine in Supporting Personal Growth

Habits and routines act as the scaffolding for building a life that resonates with our aspirations and goals. They provide a framework that supports our growth, guiding us steadily towards our ambitions.

Establishing Supportive Routines

Creating routines that back our growth initiatives involves identifying practices that align with our aspirations. These routines range from dedicating early morning hours to meditation and reflection, setting aside time for reading and learning, or even incorporating physical activities that enhance our well-being. The key lies in consistency; the daily repetition of these practices compounds over time, leading to substantial personal growth.

- **Morning Rituals:** Initiate your day with a ritual that energizes and centers you, such as meditation, exercise, or journaling. This sets a positive tone for the day ahead.
- **Learning Hour:** Allocate a specific hour for learning something new related to your growth goals. It could be reading, online courses, or practicing a skill.
- **Reflection Time:** End your day with a reflection on what you learned and achieved and how you can improve. This helps internalize the day's experiences and plan for the days ahead.

Aligning Routines with Goals

To be effective, your daily routines must be directly tied to your long-term goals. This alignment ensures that each day incrementally builds towards your ultimate objectives.

- **Goal Breakdown:** Break down your long-term goals into monthly and weekly targets. Tailor your daily routines to support these smaller milestones.

- **Visual Tracking:** Keep a visual tracker of your progress towards your goals. This could be a chart, a board, or a digital tracker that you update regularly.

Flexibility within Structure

While routines provide the necessary structure, rigidity can lead to burnout or demotivation, especially when unexpected life events occur. Incorporating flexibility within your routines ensures you can adapt without completely falling off track.

- **Buffer Time:** Incorporate buffer times in your schedule for unexpected tasks or events. This prevents your routine from being entirely disrupted by unforeseen circumstances.
- **Alternative Plans:** Have alternative routines for days when sticking to your primary routine isn't feasible. For instance, if you can't do your regular morning workout, prepare a shorter, more intense workout plan.

The Impact of Habits on Growth

The habits we cultivate play a pivotal role in our personal growth. When practiced consistently, positive habits create a virtuous cycle that propels us towards our goals. Conversely, negative habits can hinder our progress and keep us stuck in unproductive loops.

- **Positive Habit Formation:** Start with small, manageable habits contributing to your growth. For example, if your goal is to write a book, start with the habit of writing 200 words daily.
- **Replacing Negative Habits:** Identify habits holding you back and consciously replace them with positive alternatives. If mindless scrolling through social media is a time-waster for you, replace it with reading or another productive activity.

By incorporating supportive routines into our daily lives, aligning these routines with our goals, and maintaining flexibility within our structured plans, we create a conducive environment for personal growth. This approach ensures our actions are in harmony with our aspirations and equips us to navigate the unpredictability of life without losing sight of our goals. Through the mindful cultivation of positive habits and strategically replacing those that do not serve us, we harness the transformative power of our daily actions, steering ourselves steadily toward realizing our fullest potential.

6.3 Setting Goals for Your Non-Toxic Future

In pursuing a toxicity-free life, pinpointing clear, achievable objectives acts as your north star, guiding each step with purpose and intention.

The Importance of Goal Setting

Goal setting illuminates the path forward, transforming a nebulous desire for change into a tangible action plan. It's the difference between wandering aimlessly and moving with direction; it imbues your efforts with meaning and shapes your daily actions. The first step in this transformative process is recognizing that a non-toxic future is sculpted by the goals you set today.

- **Illuminate your path:** Think of each goal as a lantern in the dark, casting light on the steps ahead, making your journey towards a non-toxic future clear and navigable.
- **Shape daily actions:** Your goals determine your priorities, directly influencing how you allocate your time, energy, and resources daily.

Creating SMART Goals

SMART goals bring structure and trackability to your aspirations. They're not just wishes cast into the wind but commitments defined by their specificity, measurability, achievability, relevance, and time-bound nature.

- **Specific:** Clarify what you want to accomplish. Instead of "I want to communicate better," specify "I will express my needs directly in conversations with my partner."
- **Measurable:** Establish criteria for tracking progress. "I will express my needs in three conversations per week" gives you a tangible evaluation metric.
- **Achievable:** Ensure your goal is within reach, considering your current circumstances and constraints. It should stretch your abilities while remaining possible.

- **Relevant:** Align your goals with your broader vision for a non-toxic future. Each goal should be a building block in the life you're constructing.
- **Time-bound:** Set deadlines. "I will have these conversations over the next month" creates urgency and prompts action.

Short-term vs. Long-term Goals

Striking a balance between short-term and long-term goals ensures steady progress while maintaining sight of the ultimate vision. Short-term goals act as stepping stones, immediate targets that build momentum and foster a sense of achievement. Long-term goals, however, are the summits, the visions of your future self living a fulfilled, non-toxic life. Together, they create a ladder, with each rung propelling you upwards.

- **Stepping stones:** View short-term goals as immediate focuses that build towards your larger aspirations. Celebrate these achievements; they are signs of progress.
- **Summits:** Keep your long-term goals in sight as your guiding vision, the manifestation of your efforts and growth over time.

Adjusting Goals as You Grow

As you evolve, so too will your goals. This is natural and expected. What once seemed a distant dream may become your new starting point, and aspirations you hadn't even considered may emerge. Periodic reflection and adjustment ensure your goals remain aligned with your current self and circumstances.

- **Periodic Reflection:** Dedicate time regularly to assess your goals. Are they still in line with your vision for a non-toxic future? Have your circumstances changed, necessitating a shift in focus?
- **Adapt with Flexibility:** Allow yourself the freedom to modify your goals. This isn't a sign of failure but of growth. Your targets will naturally evolve as you learn more about yourself and what a non-toxic life looks like for you.

In setting goals for your non-toxic future, remember that this process is deeply personal and inherently flexible. Your objectives today may not be your goals tomorrow, and that's okay. What's important is that you continue to aim for what brings health, happiness, and fulfillment into your life, adjusting your course as you learn, grow, and transform. This dynamic approach to goal setting not only keeps your journey fresh and engaging but also ensures that you're always moving towards a life that truly reflects your evolved self.

6.4 The Importance of Self-Compassion in the Healing Process

In the realm of personal transformation, the act of self-compassion emerges as a light, illuminating the path toward healing and growth. This gentle approach towards oneself starkly contrasts the often harsh lens of self-criticism. Where self-criticism chains us to our past mistakes, self-compassion offers a key to our shackles, urging us towards kindness and understanding in our journey forward.

Self-compassion vs. self-criticism

At first glance, self-criticism might appear as a motivator, a strict coach pushing us to leap higher and run faster. However, its impact often veers towards the erosion of our self-esteem, leaving us feeling defeated and unworthy. Self-compassion, conversely, nurtures our spirit, encouraging growth from a place of love and acceptance. It asks us to treat ourselves with the same kindness we would offer a dear friend in distress, fostering a supportive internal environment conducive to healing and growth.

- **Impact on the psyche:** Self-criticism often leads to heightened stress and anxiety, hindering our ability to move forward. Self-compassion, on the other hand, reduces these negative emotional states, creating a sense of safety from which we can explore and grow.
- **Influence on behavior:** Where self-criticism can paralyze us with fear of failure, self-compassion encourages risk-taking and exploration, essential components of personal development.

Practicing self-compassion

The art of self-compassion can be cultivated through intentional practice, weaving it into the fabric of our daily lives. Mindfulness stands as a cornerstone in this practice, asking us to observe our thoughts and emotions without judgment. Self-kindness exercises further enrich this practice, allowing us to replace critical or harmful thoughts with ones of understanding and care.

- **Mindfulness exercises:** Engage in daily mindfulness meditation, focusing on breathing and bodily sensations, to enhance awareness of the present moment and reduce negative self-judgment.
- **Self-kindness affirmations:** Incorporate affirmations that reinforce self-worth and acceptance. Phrases such as "I am doing my best, and that is enough" can be powerful antidotes to self-critical thoughts.

The role of self-compassion in resilience

Resilience, the ability to bounce back from adversity, is significantly bolstered by self-compassion. It offers a wellspring of emotional resilience, equipping us with the inner strength to face challenges without succumbing to despair or self-doubt. Self-compassion ensures that when we stumble, we are met with a supportive internal dialogue that encourages perseverance rather than condemnation.

- **Enhancing emotional flexibility:** Self-compassion promotes emotional flexibility, allowing us to navigate setbacks with grace and adaptability.
- **Supporting sustainable growth:** By fostering an internal environment marked by kindness and encouragement, self-compassion ensures that our journey toward personal growth is sustainable and grounded in positive self-regard.

Forgiving yourself for past toxic behavior

An integral aspect of self-compassion in the healing process is the act of self-forgiveness. It requires us to acknowledge our past toxic behaviors not as definitions of our character but as actions borne from a place of unawareness or pain. Forgiving ourselves liberates us from the chains of past mistakes, opening the door to a future where we can embody our highest selves.

- **Acknowledgment and acceptance:** Begin by acknowledging the toxic behaviors and accepting that they were part of your path.

This acknowledgment is not an excuse but a step towards understanding and healing.
- **Self-forgiveness exercises:** Engage in exercises that foster self-forgiveness, such as writing letters to yourself expressing forgiveness and understanding. These exercises can be powerful tools for releasing guilt and fostering a compassionate relationship with oneself.

The journey towards healing and personal growth is enriched immeasurably by the practice of self-compassion. By choosing to approach ourselves with kindness, understanding, and forgiveness, we create an internal landscape where growth is not just possible but inevitable. This compassionate stance towards ourselves ensures that the path forward is marked not by self-criticism and guilt but by love, resilience, and an unwavering belief in our capacity for change and healing. Through self-compassion, we not only heal the wounds of our past but also cultivate a future replete with emotional health, fulfillment, and an ever-deepening sense of self-love.

6.5 Building a Personal Growth Plan: Short and Long-Term Strategies

A personal growth plan serves as your roadmap, offering clarity and direction as you navigate the complexities of self-improvement. It is a tool that ensures your efforts are aligned, focused, and reflect your ultimate goals. This plan is not static; it evolves as you do, continually adapting to reflect your current aspirations, challenges, and achievements.

The Importance of a Personal Growth Plan

Creating a personal growth plan is like plotting a course before setting sail. Without it, you're adrift, subject to the whims of circumstance and fleeting motivation. With it, you have a clear destination, and every action takes on purpose, propelling you forward. This plan solidifies your commitment to growth as a tangible reminder of your journey's purpose and the steps necessary to realize your vision.

Components of a Personal Growth Plan

An effective personal growth plan comprises several essential elements, each contributing to a holistic strategy for personal development. These components include:

- **Vision Statement:** Begin with a broad vision for your life. This could encompass career aspirations, personal development goals, and the qualities you wish to embody. The vision statement should inspire and motivate, serving as the guiding light for your growth journey.
- **Specific Goals:** Break down your vision into achievable goals. These should be concrete, measurable, and tied directly to your overarching vision. For instance, if part of your vision involves leading a healthier lifestyle, specific goals might include running a 5K or incorporating vegetables into every meal.
- **Action Steps:** For each goal, outline specific actions or steps required to achieve it. These steps make your goals actionable, transforming lofty aspirations into manageable tasks. If your goal is to run a 5K, action steps might include a weekly training schedule and a plan for gradually increasing your distance.
- **Resources and Tools:** Identify the resources and tools that will support your growth. This might include books, courses, apps, or even mentors and coaches. Acknowledging these resources upfront ensures you have the support needed to achieve your goals.
- **Timeline:** Establish a timeline for your goals, including both short-term milestones and long-term targets. This helps maintain momentum and provides regular checkpoints to assess progress.

Balancing Short-term and Long-term Strategies

A balanced growth plan harmonizes immediate actions with your future vision, ensuring that today's efforts contribute to tomorrow's achievements. This balance prevents the common pitfalls of becoming too focused on distant aspirations at the expense of present action or, conversely, getting caught up in day-to-day tasks without a clear direction for the future.

- **Integrate Daily Practices:** Incorporate practices into your daily routine that align with both your immediate and long-term goals. For example, a daily practice of journaling can improve self-awareness (a short-term benefit) while contributing to emotional intelligence over time (a long-term goal).
- **Regular Check-ins:** Schedule regular reviews of your plan. This might be weekly, monthly, or quarterly, depending on your goals.

Use these check-ins to celebrate progress, adjust strategies, and realign your actions with your overarching vision.

Reviewing and Adjusting Your Plan

Flexibility is a cornerstone of any personal growth plan. Life is unpredictable, and your interests, circumstances, and goals will evolve. Regular reviews of your plan are critical to ensure it remains relevant and aligned with your current self.

- **Reflect on Progress and Challenges:** Use your check-ins to reflect on what's working and what isn't. Celebrate the progress you've made and consider any obstacles you've encountered. This reflection can provide valuable insights for adjusting your plan.
- **Adjust Goals as Needed:** Don't hesitate to modify your goals based on new insights, achievements, or shifts in your priorities. Growth is a dynamic process, and your plan should be equally adaptable.
- **Seek Feedback:** Sometimes, an outside perspective can offer new insights into your growth journey. Don't shy away from seeking feedback from trusted friends, mentors, or coaches. Use this feedback to refine and enhance your plan.

In constructing a personal growth plan that balances short-term actions with long-term visions and remains adaptable to life's inevitable changes, you create a powerful tool for intentional self-improvement. This plan becomes your compass, guiding your decisions and actions with purpose and clarity. Through regular reflection and adjustment, your personal growth plan evolves alongside you, ensuring that your journey of self-improvement is both meaningful and aligned with your deepest aspirations.

6.6 Maintaining Healthy Boundaries as You Grow

As we develop and evolve, so do our needs and sense of self. This natural progression impacts our inner landscape and how we interact with the world around us. A critical aspect of this interaction is establishing and adjusting personal boundaries. These invisible lines define what we are comfortable with, what we value, and how we allow others to treat us. As such, they are not static but dynamic, changing as we change, reflecting our current state of being and understanding.

The Evolving Nature of Boundaries

Initially, our boundaries might be broad, designed more for exploration than protection. However, as we grow, we learn what matters most to us, what we're willing to accept, and what we must refuse to sustain our well-being. This clarity comes from a deeper understanding of our values, desires, and the kind of life we wish to lead. Recognizing that our boundaries will shift is vital; it means we are attentive to our evolving needs and are committed to honoring them. Regularly reassessing these boundaries ensures they remain in alignment with our current selves, serving us adequately.

- Reflect on experiences that have shaped or shifted your priorities and values.
- Periodically review your boundaries, asking if they still serve your best interests and reflect your current understanding of yourself.

Communicating Changing Boundaries

As our boundaries shift, articulating these changes to others becomes crucial. Clear communication not only helps maintain healthy relationships but also reinforces our commitment to self-respect and personal growth. It involves expressing our needs and limits assertively, without apologizing but respecting the other person's autonomy.

- Use "I" statements to convey your boundaries, focusing on your feelings and needs rather than placing blame or making demands.
- Be direct and clear, avoiding ambiguity that could lead to misunderstandings.
- Practice in low-stakes situations to build confidence in communicating more significant boundary shifts.

Boundaries and Self-Respect

The act of setting and maintaining boundaries is deeply intertwined with self-respect. It signals a commitment to oneself, acknowledging that our feelings, needs, and comfort matter. This respect for self acts as the bedrock upon which healthy relationships are built, as it teaches others how we expect to be treated based on how we treat ourselves. When we uphold our boundaries, we affirm our worth, reinforcing the idea that we deserve to be treated with respect and kindness.

- Recognize that upholding your boundaries is an act of self-love.
- Understand that respecting your boundaries encourages others to do the same, fostering mutual respect in relationships.

Protecting Your Energy

As we become more open and vulnerable in our growth journey, safeguarding our energy becomes paramount. Our energy is finite, and where we choose to invest, it can significantly impact our well-being and progress. Boundaries play a critical role in this protection, acting as filters that allow us to decide what deserves our time, attention, and emotional investment.

- Learn to identify situations and interactions that drain your energy and consider setting stricter boundaries in these areas.
- Give yourself permission to step back or disengage from energy-draining circumstances, understanding that doing so is not selfish but necessary for your well-being.
- Explore practices that replenish your energy, such as spending time in nature, engaging in creative activities, or practicing meditation, and prioritize these in your routine.

In navigating the complexities of personal growth, understanding that our boundaries will and should evolve alongside us is crucial. This evolution requires not just recognition but action—clear communication of our changing needs, a steadfast commitment to self-respect, and vigilant protection of our energy. As we adjust our boundaries to reflect our current state of being, we facilitate healthier interactions, deeper connections, and a more authentic expression of ourselves. This process, while challenging, is essential for maintaining balance and harmony in our lives as we continue to grow and change.

6.7 Celebrating Your Non-Toxic Identity and Embracing the Future

In the landscape of self-improvement, acknowledging the strides we've made in shedding toxic behaviors and adopting healthier habits marks a crucial milestone. This recognition serves not as a final destination but as a vantage point, offering a panoramic view of both the ground covered and the paths yet to be traversed.

Recognizing your transformation

The transition from toxic behaviors to healthier habits and mindsets is akin to the metamorphosis of a caterpillar into a butterfly. It's a profound change that touches every aspect of our being. Paying homage to this transformation involves more than a cursory glance at where we started versus where we stand today. It entails an in-depth reflection on the shifts in our thoughts, behaviors, and interactions with others. These changes, regardless of their magnitude, deserve celebration. They are testaments to our resilience, determination, and growth.

- Reflect on the contrasts between your past and present self, acknowledging the efforts and sacrifices made along the way.
- Celebrate these changes with rituals that hold personal significance, whether that's a quiet moment of gratitude or sharing your story with others.

The ongoing journey

Personal growth is not a linear process with a clear beginning and end. It's an ongoing cycle of learning, evolving, and adapting. Embracing this journey with an open heart and a curious mind allows us to remain flexible and responsive to life's inevitable shifts. This openness ensures that we continue to grow in alignment with our deepest values and aspirations, even as they evolve.

- Stay curious about yourself and the world around you, viewing each day as an opportunity to learn something new.
- Embrace the fluid nature of personal growth, understanding that change is inevitable and beneficial.

Setting visions for the future

As we move forward, setting visions for our future that mirror our non-toxic identity and aspirations becomes crucial. These visions are not rigid blueprints but flexible guides shaped by our deepest desires and highest aspirations.

- Envision a future that resonates with your values and aspirations, allowing this vision to guide your decisions and actions.
- Consider the roles you wish to play, the experiences you desire, and the impact you hope to have, weaving these elements into your vision for the future.

Embracing change with confidence

Looking ahead, we will encounter changes and challenges that will test our resilience and determination. Embracing these changes with confidence and the knowledge that we possess the tools and resilience to navigate them allows us to face the future with optimism and strength. Our journey thus far has equipped us with invaluable insights and skills, preparing us to meet future challenges head-on.

- Trust in your ability to adapt and thrive in the face of change, drawing on the lessons and strengths you've developed.
- Approach future changes and challenges with a proactive mindset, viewing them as opportunities for further growth and learning.

As we draw this chapter to a close, let us take a moment to reflect on the essence of our journey. From recognizing the profound transformation we've undergone, embracing the ongoing nature of personal growth, setting visionary goals for our non-toxic future, and facing changes with unwavering confidence, our path is marked by continuous evolution and boundless potential. As we step into the next phase of our journey, let us carry forward the lessons learned, the strengths honed, and the visions crafted, ready to explore new horizons with courage, curiosity, and an open heart.

7

BEYOND THE MIRROR: EXTENDING YOUR IMPACT

A pebble dropped in a still pond creates ripples that travel far beyond its initial impact. Similarly, the changes you make in your life resonate beyond your immediate environment, influencing those around you in subtle yet profound ways. This chapter explores how personal transformation extends its reach, touching the lives of others and fostering a culture of positivity and growth. It's not just about the transformation within but how this transformation becomes a catalyst for wider change, creating a ripple effect that encourages a healthier, more supportive environment for everyone.

7.1 The Ripple Effect: How Your Change Affects Others

Understanding the ripple effect

Think about the last time someone's positive mood lifted your spirits or how a colleague's dedication inspired you to put extra effort into your work. These instances are everyday examples of the ripple effect in action. Changes in your behavior, attitude, and approach to life don't exist in a vacuum. They send out waves that can either uplift or dampen the spirits of those around you. Recognizing this interconnectedness highlights the broader impact of personal growth.

Modeling positive behavior

When you decide to replace a habit of snapping at your partner with one of expressing needs calmly, you're not just improving your relationship. You're also demonstrating healthier communication practices. Over time, this can encourage your partner to adopt a similar approach, improving how you both handle disagreements. The same principle applies in the workplace. Opting to tackle challenges with a positive outlook can inspire a shift in the team's approach to problem-solving, fostering a more collaborative and innovative atmosphere.

- **Real-life scenario:** At your next team meeting, highlight the progress made instead of focusing on the hurdles. This subtle shift in focus can boost morale and encourage a more solution-oriented mindset among your colleagues.

The power of positive reinforcement

Acknowledging and reinforcing the positive behaviors of those around you is a powerful motivator. It's the principle of positive reinforcement in psychology—rewarding behavior increases the likelihood of it being repeated. So, when you notice a family member making an effort to be more patient or a coworker taking initiative, a simple acknowledgment can go a long way.

- **When and how:** During a family dinner, point out and appreciate the patience your sibling showed in teaching their child a new skill. In the workplace, a quick email thanking a colleague for their proactive approach can reinforce their behavior.

Navigating resistance to change

Change can be unsettling, and not everyone in your circle may welcome your transformation, especially if it challenges the status quo. Some might prefer the familiarity of old habits, while others might feel implicitly criticized by your growth. This resistance requires a delicate balance of empathy and firmness in your commitment to positive change.

- **Strategy for resistance:** Keep your communication open and centered on your experience. For example, if a friend resists your new approach to handling conflict, explain your reasons and the positive outcomes you've noticed rather than criticizing their methods.

7.2 Creating a Non-Toxic Environment at Home and Work

When we turn our attention to the spaces we inhabit most—our homes and workplaces—we uncover the profound influence these environments have on our mental and emotional well-being. The act of cultivating non-toxic spaces is akin to tending a garden. Just as a gardener nurtures the soil, plants seeds with care, and diligently weeds, so too must we assess, curate, and maintain our personal and professional spaces to support our growth and happiness.

Assessing Your Environment

The first step in this process involves a thoughtful evaluation of your current surroundings. This means taking stock of the dynamics at play within your home and workplace. Are conversations generally supportive or critical? Do the physical spaces invite relaxation and creativity, or do they contribute to stress and discomfort? Identifying the sources of negativity is critical before you can begin to introduce positive changes.

- Start by listing the aspects of your home and work environment that you find draining or stressful.
- Conversely, note the elements that bring you joy and energy, as these are what you'll aim to amplify.

Setting Boundaries for a Healthy Environment

Boundaries are the protective fences that safeguard our well-being. In both home and work contexts, clear boundaries help prevent the encroachment of negativity into our spaces. At home, this might look like setting specific times for work and rest, ensuring that the stresses of the job don't bleed into family time. In the workplace, it might involve setting clear expectations around communication, such as no work emails after a certain hour, to respect personal time and mental health.

- For home: Establish 'quiet hours' where all household members

agree to respect each other's need for peace, whether for work, study, or relaxation.
- For work: Advocate for regular check-ins where team members can voice concerns and suggestions in a constructive manner, promoting a culture of open communication and mutual respect.

Implementing Changes Gradually

Radical changes often meet resistance, both from within us and from those around us. Introducing modifications to our environments gradually allows for a smoother transition and greater acceptance. This could mean starting with small, manageable changes, like reorganizing your workspace for better functionality or introducing a weekly family meeting to discuss everyone's needs and concerns. Over time, these small adjustments can lead to significant positive shifts in the overall atmosphere of your home and workplace.

- Initiate a single change each week, allowing yourself and others to adapt and find comfort in these new practices before introducing additional changes.

Engaging Others in the Process

Creating a non-toxic environment is seldom a solitary endeavor. It requires the buy-in and participation of everyone involved. At home, this might involve family discussions where each member can voice their ideas and concerns about creating a more harmonious living space. At work, consider collaborative sessions where team members can share their insights on improving the office environment. This inclusive approach not only ensures that changes are broadly supported but also fosters a collective commitment to maintaining a positive atmosphere.

- For family: Hold a monthly 'family council' where everyone can suggest one change they believe would improve the home environment.
- For work: Organize a 'positive change brainstorm' session with colleagues to identify practical steps towards a healthier workplace.

The endeavor to foster non-toxic spaces at home and work is a testament to the belief that our environments play a crucial role in our well-being and growth. Through careful assessment, the establishment of thoughtful boundaries, gradual implementation of changes, and the engagement of those who share our spaces, we lay the groundwork for environments that not only support but actively contribute to our journey towards a healthier, more fulfilled self.

7.3 Encouraging Non-Toxic Behavior in Others

The transformation towards a non-toxic lifestyle extends beyond self-improvement; it also involves fostering environments where others feel inspired to adopt similar behaviors. This section outlines strategies for encouraging positive change in those around us, emphasizing the significance of leading by example, the use of positive reinforcement, the creation of growth opportunities, and constructive approaches to handling setbacks.

Leading by Example

The most powerful tool at our disposal is our own behavior. Actions often speak louder than words, making our conduct a potent means of inspiring change. When we consistently demonstrate patience, understanding, and respect in our interactions, we not only create a more harmonious environment but also set a standard for others to aspire to.

- In situations where tensions may rise, choose to respond with calmness and empathy. This approach can diffuse potential conflicts and serve as a model for constructive communication.
- Share your experiences and the positive outcomes of your behavior changes. Hearing about tangible benefits can motivate others to consider similar adjustments in their actions.

Positive Reinforcement Techniques

Acknowledging and rewarding non-toxic behavior in others can significantly reinforce these actions, encouraging their recurrence. Positive reinforcement creates an environment where positive actions are noticed and valued, increasing their frequency.

- Offer genuine compliments when you notice someone making an effort to change a behavior. For instance, if a coworker handles a stressful situation with grace, acknowledge their approach with specific praise.
- Public recognition can also be a powerful motivator. Recognizing someone's efforts in a group setting, such as during a family gathering or a team meeting, can amplify the impact of positive reinforcement.

Creating Opportunities for Growth

Cultivating a culture that encourages personal and collective growth can foster non-toxic behaviors. Creating spaces where individuals feel safe to express themselves, learn from each other, and explore their potential can lead to profound transformations.

- Organize group activities focused on developing emotional intelligence, such as workshops or discussion groups. These can provide valuable tools for understanding and managing emotions, benefiting everyone involved.
- Encourage collaborative projects at work or within the family that require teamwork and open communication. These projects can teach the value of diverse perspectives and the strength found in working together towards a common goal.

Addressing Setbacks Constructively

Setbacks are inevitable in any process of change. When they occur, focusing on what can be learned rather than assigning blame fosters a resilient and supportive environment. This approach encourages individuals to view setbacks as part of the growth process, not as failures.

- When someone regresses to a toxic behavior, approach the situation with empathy. Discuss what might have triggered the setback and explore strategies for better handling similar situations in the future.
- Promote a mindset that views mistakes as learning opportunities. This can help reduce the fear of failure and encourage a more open and experimental approach to personal development.

By leading by example, employing positive reinforcement, creating opportunities for growth, and addressing setbacks constructively, we can significantly influence the behaviors of those around us. These strategies not only encourage the adoption of non-toxic behaviors but also contribute to the creation of environments where everyone is supported in their pursuit of personal growth and well-being.

7.4 Coping with Setbacks Without Reverting to Old Patterns

When strides towards non-toxic living meet obstacles, it's a moment ripe for introspection rather than despair. Such instances aren't detours on the path of personal transformation but integral parts of the landscape itself. Accepting that setbacks are natural helps dismantle the illusion of a faultless progression toward betterment. This realization is vital, as it cushions the impact of challenges and reframes them as opportunities for deeper understanding and growth.

In navigating these inevitable hurdles, resilience becomes our ally. This resilience isn't innate but cultivated through practices that fortify our mental and emotional fortitude. Strategies for nurturing this resilience include:

- **Self-reflection:** This practice involves looking inward to understand the root causes of setbacks. It's about asking ourselves honest questions about our actions, thoughts, and the external factors contributing to the situation. This process requires patience and the willingness to confront uncomfortable truths about ourselves and our circumstances.
- **Seeking support:** The journey towards non-toxic living isn't meant to be solitary. Reaching out for support, be it from friends, family, or professionals, provides perspective, encouragement, and practical advice. This network acts as a sounding board, offering insights that might not be apparent from our viewpoint.
- **Adjusting strategies as needed:** Flexibility in our approach allows us to pivot and adapt in the face of setbacks. This might mean revising our goals, trying new methods, or even temporarily stepping back to recharge. The key is to view these adjustments not as concessions but as strategic moves that keep us aligned with our overarching goals.

Learning from setbacks transforms them from perceived failures into valuable lessons. This learning process involves:

- Identifying patterns: Recognizing recurring themes in setbacks can reveal underlying issues that need addressing. For instance, if impatience frequently derails efforts to communicate effectively, focusing on developing patience becomes a priority.
- Extracting lessons: Each setback holds lessons on what works, what doesn't, and why. Reflecting on these lessons helps refine our approach, making us better equipped to handle similar situations in the future.
- Applying insights: The true value of these lessons lies in their application. Integrating newfound understanding into our actions and strategies enhances our ability to navigate challenges more adeptly.

Maintaining motivation amidst setbacks is crucial for continued progress. Strategies for sustaining this motivation include:

- Celebrating small wins: Recognizing and celebrating even minor victories along the way fuels our drive to persist. These celebrations act as reminders of our capability and progress, bolstering our resolve to move forward.
- Revisiting our why: Reminding ourselves of the reasons behind our pursuit of non-toxic living can reignite our motivation. Whether it's for personal well-being, healthier relationships, or a more fulfilling life, reconnecting with our core motivations provides clarity and renews our commitment.
- Visualizing success: Imagining ourselves achieving our goals, free from the patterns that once held us back, can be a powerful motivator. This visualization not only uplifts our spirits but also toughens our determination to overcome the obstacles in our path.

In sum, coping with setbacks without falling back into old patterns demands acceptance, resilience, and the willingness to learn and adapt. It's about grounding ourselves in the reality that challenges are part of growth, seeking support when the going gets tough, and keeping our eyes on the prize, even when the road there seems fraught with hurdles. Through self-reflection, embracing flexibility, learning from each bump, and keeping our motivation alive, we navigate these setbacks not as hindrances but as stepping stones to a richer, more authentic life.

7.5 The Role of Forgiveness in Overcoming Toxicity

Forgiveness stands as a pillar in the architecture of healing, a necessary step towards liberating oneself from the chains of past grievances. It's a process that involves a deep dive into understanding, acceptance, and, ultimately, release. This chapter unfolds the significance of forgiveness, not just as an act of mercy towards others but as a crucial component of self-care and personal development.

Forgiveness is often misunderstood. It does not imply overlooking or excusing harmful actions. Instead, it signifies a conscious decision to let go of resentment and thoughts of revenge. This emotional release does not validate wrongdoing but frees the individual from an endless cycle of anger and bitterness, thus allowing space for healing and growth.

The Importance of Forgiveness

The act of forgiving both oneself and others is a cornerstone in the foundation of emotional wellness. It's akin to clearing the weeds from a garden, allowing new, healthy growth to take place. Without forgiveness, we remain tethered to the past, hindering our ability to move forward and embrace the possibilities that lie ahead.

- Forgiveness is not a sign of weakness but of strength. It demonstrates a profound understanding of human fallibility and the capacity for compassion.
- By releasing the hold that past hurts have on us, we open ourselves to healing, leading to improved mental and emotional health.

Forgiving Without Condoning

Understanding the distinction between forgiving and condoning is crucial. To forgive does not mean to forget or to give a free pass to unacceptable behavior. It means acknowledging the pain caused yet choosing to break free from its grip on your emotional well-being.

- This differentiation allows one to hold others accountable for their actions while still letting go of the anger and resentment that serve no constructive purpose.

Steps to Forgiveness

Navigating the path to forgiveness can be complex, requiring patience and persistence. Here are steps to guide you through this transformative process:

1. **Acknowledge the Hurt:** Confront the emotions tied to the experience. Allow yourself to feel anger, sadness, or betrayal without judgment.
2. **Empathize with the Other Party:** Attempt to understand the circumstances or motivations behind the other person's actions. This does not excuse their behavior but can provide context that aids in the process of forgiveness.
3. **Consciously Choose to Forgive:** Make a deliberate decision to forgive. This choice is for your peace of mind and emotional liberation, not for the benefit of the other person.
4. **Express Forgiveness:** Whether verbally, in writing, or silently within your heart, articulate your forgiveness. This expression marks a significant step in releasing the emotional burden.

Forgiveness as a Tool for Growth

Embracing forgiveness paves the way for profound personal growth. It shifts the focus from past grievances to future aspirations, allowing us to engage with life from a place of understanding and peace.

- Forgiveness strengthens relationships by promoting empathy and compassion. It fosters a climate of trust and mutual respect, which is essential for healthy, supportive interactions.
- On a personal level, forgiveness contributes to emotional maturity. It teaches us about the complexity of human behavior and our capacity for empathy, resilience, and love.

In a world that often emphasizes holding onto grievances as a form of emotional armor, choosing forgiveness is a radical act. It signifies a commitment to one's mental and emotional freedom, a step towards a life unburdened by the weight of past hurts. Through forgiveness, we reclaim our power, redirecting our emotional energy toward nurturing positivity, growth, and meaningful connections.

As we close this chapter, it's clear that forgiveness, both of oneself and of others, is a vital element in overcoming toxicity. It's a journey that requires understanding, empathy, and a conscious choice to release the past. This process not only heals old wounds but also lays the groundwork for a future filled with potential, growth, and deeper connections. In the chapters that follow, we will continue to explore avenues for personal transformation, building upon the foundation of forgiveness to cultivate a life marked by health, happiness, and fulfillment.

I WOULD LOVE TO HEAR FROM YOU

If you found value in this book, I kindly ask for your review and for you to share your experience with others. Please take a moment to leave a review on Amazon and share how this book has impacted your path to personal growth.

Your feedback not only helps me, but it also guides others in their journey towards change. It's through your support and reviews that my book is able to reach the hands of other readers.

Please take 60 seconds to kindly leave a review on Amazon.
If you reside outside of US, please use the link in your order.

All it takes is 60 seconds to make a difference!

CONCLUSION

As we reach the culmination of this profound journey, it's essential to pause and reflect on the path we have traversed together. You embarked on this voyage with the courage to confront the shadows within, to acknowledge and address the toxic behaviors that have hindered your growth and relationships. This book has guided you through the labyrinth of self-awareness, emotional intelligence, effective communication, and the myriad strategies to overcome obstacles and sustain meaningful change. Your dedication to unraveling the roots of toxic behavior, cultivating empathy, setting healthy boundaries, and engaging in continuous self-improvement is commendable. These are not mere steps on a path but leaps toward becoming a more authentic, compassionate, and resilient individual.

Understanding the deep-seated origins of toxic behaviors, embracing emotional intelligence, and practicing effective communication are pivotal achievements. The value of empathy, self-compassion, and resilience cannot be overstated, for they are the bedrock upon which lasting transformation is built. Every effort you have made, every insight gained, and every boundary set is a testament to your commitment to shedding the weight of toxicity and fostering healthier, more fulfilling connections.

The courage it takes to face oneself, to dismantle long-held patterns of harm, and to step into a space of vulnerability and growth is truly remarkable. It is a victory in itself, deserving of recognition and celebration.

Conclusion

The road to self-improvement does not end here. I urge you to keep the momentum alive, to continually engage in self-reflection, and to embrace the inevitable ebbs and flows of personal growth with patience and grace. The strategies and insights shared within these pages are tools in your arsenal, ready to be wielded as you navigate the complexities of life and relationships. Remember, you have already taken the first step when you picked up this book, and you can return to it time and again for guidance, reassurance, and motivation.

Setbacks and relapses are not failures but signposts, indicating areas for further exploration and growth. They are part of change, woven into the very process of self-improvement. Embrace these moments with kindness and curiosity, for they hold valuable lessons that pave the way for deeper understanding and resilience.

In closing, I want to leave you with these words of encouragement: You possess boundless inner strength and capacity for change. The future that lies ahead is bright, with the promise of growth, deeper connections, and a life free from the constraints of toxicity. Embrace your journey with hope, determination, and grace, and discover your most authentic selves. Remember, you are not alone. Together, we walk towards a horizon filled with light, compassion, and endless possibilities.

ALSO BY TAYLOR BLAKE

8-Week Couples Relationship Therapy Workbook

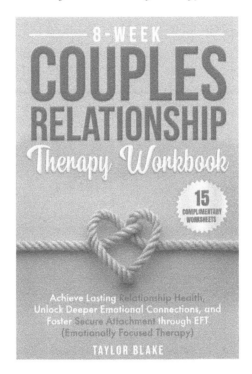

REFERENCES

Top 11 Benefits of Self-Awareness According to Science https://positivepsychology.com/benefits-of-self-awareness/

Why Toxic People Are So Harmful | Psychology Today https://www.psychologytoday.com/us/blog/here-there-and-everywhere/202306/why-toxic-people-are-so-harmful#:~:text=They%20Negatively%20Impact%20Your%20Mental%20and%20Physical%20Health&text=Constant%20criticism%20and%20belittlement%20can,of%20loneliness%20and%20social%20withdrawal.

Toxic, Dysfunctional Behavior Patterns and How to Recognize Them https://trustmentalhealth.com/blog/toxic-dysfunctional-behavior-patterns-and-how-to-recognize-them

Manipulation-GoodTherapy https://www.goodtherapy.org/blog/psychpedia/manipulation/#:~:text=A%20counselor%20may%20also%20be,be%20contributing%20to%20the%20behavior.

The Importance of Self-Introspection: A Path to Personal ... https://www.linkedin.com/pulse/importance-self-introspection-path-personal-growth-avik-debnath-hgpfc

How to Develop Emotional Intelligence Skills https://online.hbs.edu/blog/post/emotional-intelligence-skills

DBT Mindfulness Exercises to Regulate Emotions https://eddinscounseling.com/dbt-mindfulness-exercises/

Cultivating empathy - American Psychological Association https://www.apa.org/monitor/2021/11/feature-cultivating-empathy

Active Listening in Relationships: A Path To Deeper Intimacy https://holdinghopemft.com/active-listening-a-key-to-deeper-intimacy-and-understanding-in-your-relationship/

Effective Communication For Conflict Resolution https://www.aifc.com.au/effective-communication-for-conflict-resolution/

6 Steps to Rebuilding Trust After Betrayal https://www.psychologytoday.com/us/blog/hope-relationships/202205/6-steps-rebuilding-trust-after-betrayal

Vulnerability in Relationships: Benefits and Tips https://psychcentral.com/relationships/trust-and-vulnerability-in-relationships

Constructive Criticism: A Key to Personal and Professional ... https://www.larksuite.com/en_us/topics/productivity-glossary/constructive-criticism

Understanding and Overcoming the Fear of Vulnerability https://www.linkedin.com/pulse/understanding-overcoming-fear-vulnerability-muhibullah-sahibjan#:~:text=Overcoming%20fear%20of%20vulnerability%20is,trust%20in%20yourself%20and%20others.

Staying Motivated During Challenging Times - LinkedIn https://www.linkedin.com/pulse/staying-motivated-during-challenging-times-strategies-angle-young

Caring for Your Mental Health https://www.nimh.nih.gov/health/topics/caring-for-your-mental-health#:~:text=Self%2Dcare%20means%20taking%20the,illness%2C%20and%20increase%20your%20energy.

SMART Goals - How to Make Your Goals Achievable https://www.mindtools.com/a4wo118/smart-goals

21 Mindfulness Exercises & Activities For Adults (+ PDF) https://positivepsychology.com/mindfulness-exercises-techniques-activities/

The Benefits of Self-Compassion in Mental Health ... https://www.ncbi.nlm.nih.gov/pmc/articles/PMC9482966/